WOMEN, LEADERSHIP, and SAVING the WORLD

WHY EVERYTHING GETS BETTER WHEN WOMEN LEAD

info@womensleadershipintensive.ca

ISBN: 978-1-7386588-0-0 (paperback)
ISBN: 978-1-7386588-1-7 (ebook)

Ordering Information:
Special discounts are available on quantity purchases by corporations, associations, and others. For details, contact info@womensleadershipintensive.ca.

WOMEN, LEADERSHIP, and SAVING the WORLD

WHY EVERYTHING GETS BETTER WHEN WOMEN LEAD

BELINDA CLEMMENSEN

This book is dedicated to all the women thought leaders, organizers, advocates and freedom fighters who went before us. All the women who are waking up, standing up and raising their voices today, and perhaps most especially to the young people, girls and boys, growing up in generations to come. May we make the road easier and more equitable so they can achieve their greatest potential. The world needs them so.

Who am I to write a book about women's leadership?

You know, I've asked myself that question so many times. I've asked in the deep sense of the question: Who am I and what am I here to do? That's the real question we all have. And I've asked in the imposter syndrome sense of the word: Who do I think I am to write this book or any book? But I keep coming up with the same answer. If I am a leader, then I need to try. I need to get past the self-doubt, say what I think and know that it won't be perfect and that some folks won't like it or agree with it. So be it.

I also need to accept that any book about gender equality and women in leadership will be representative only of this moment in time. Our conversations and understanding of equality, equity and gender are changing daily. And that's a good thing. My own thinking on these topics is growing and changing daily—also good.

Where I'm coming from is a lifetime of observing the dynamics between and among genders in our world, both on the small scale of my own life and circles and on the global stage through reviewing research, reading articles and observing who leads what in our world.

I've taken university-level courses on feminist theory, written and published papers on gender differences in the professions I've worked in and spent a career learning and teaching leadership development around the world. Besides that, I've been a seeker, looking for meaning and understanding in my own life and life in general.

There were two formative experiences that taught me the most about leadership and about women in leadership in particular. The first began in the year 2000. I was 30 years old and already tired from my experiences of being a woman in leadership. I was working in the outdoor and experiential leadership field, doing both organizational training and development, and leading wilderness expeditions (mostly sea kayaking trips, my passion). I wanted to try something different than what I had experienced and co-create an expedition that was by women, for women and was built on the principles of community, contribution, inclusion, accessibility and sharing of power. Paddle to a Cure: Journeys of Hope was a series of sea kayaking expeditions that would both raise money for breast cancer research and education and take those dealing with the illness into the Canadian wilderness for a healing experience with a community of support. I knew the healing power of the wilderness firsthand, and I believed it would make a difference.

We began, myself and three other talented outdoor leaders, Sarah

Oosterhuis, Ally Myers and Annie Myers. We wanted to take the summer of 2000 and raise as much money as we could while taking great care of our participants and creating a unique outdoor experience. We did that. It was both tough and magical. There are so many moments from that first year that are burned into my memory. It was life changing. At the end of that summer, our participants started asking us about the next year. We hadn't thought about a next year. But we said yes, and five years later we had raised almost a million dollars for breast cancer and taken hundreds of participants into the wilderness across Canada. It was beautiful. And it was completely led by women.

We did leadership very differently than I'd ever seen it done before. We led as a community, and we led by our values, even when it was hard, even when it would have been way easier to default to other ways of leading. That taught me a lot. It taught me that there are different ways to build and lead organizations and that women working together intentionally do things differently, and that is a good thing. A great thing. To this day, many of the friendships and working relationships built over those five years are the strongest and most supportive I've ever seen. We've been together through births, deaths and everything in between. We show up. And we still go to the wilderness to paddle together, laugh, play and heal.

The second big experience happened almost 20 years later. I was humming along with my leadership development business, working with organizations and, for the most part, feeling pretty good about the work I was doing. Sure, I didn't always feel values aligned with the decisions some of my client companies were making. Sure, I noticed that not everyone was treated equally or equitably. But I comforted myself by saying I was there to try to make things better for the people in those organizations. And that worked, until it didn't. I started to feel like I was supporting a machine that I didn't quite believe in. Call it modern capitalism, call it the patriarchy, call it business, whatever. What I knew was that I could no longer convince myself that the work I was doing was enough to truly make the kind of difference that really mattered to me.

I went into a time of uncertainty. I decided to start by just observing. I had to keep working because I had bills to pay. I worked, and I noticed how each project felt. And week by week, month by month, I'd drive home from a project, and I'd think to myself, *No. Not that. That's not really what I want to be doing with my life.* The question was: What *did* I want to do with it? I felt limited by developing leaders according to the boundaries of corporate expectations. It often felt like my hands were tied and I couldn't dive into the deep conversations about what it really means to be a leader—well beyond the job title. It was a good friend and colleague, Tim Arnold, who called me home to my core, women in leadership. He reminded me of my passion, my life experiences, the research, and everything I knew about the difference women in leadership make in our communities, organizations and world. And I realized that if I truly wanted to support leaders, women were the ones I wanted to support. And the Women's Leadership Intensive was born, with our mission to inspire, empower, support and equip women to lead the change the world needs.

And the rest is history. No, just kidding. The rest is written here in this book. I hope the story of women in leadership draws you in and draws you forward into action, as much as it has for me. An optimist at my core, it is my firm belief that women in leadership are a key lever in saving our world from the complex local and global challenges we face today. I hope this book will feed that optimism and belief in you too.

In the future, women, rather than men, will be the ones to change the world.

— MALALA YOUSAFZAI[1]

As long as outmoded ways of thinking prevent women from making a meaningful contribution to society, progress will be slow.

— NELSON MANDELA[2]

---

1   Maria Rioumine, "Malala Yousafzai's Toughest Battle?" Huffington Post, updated February 12, 2014, https://www.huffpost.com/entry/malala-yousafzais-toughes_b_4435517.

2   "Speech by President Nelson Mandela on Women's Day, Pretoria, 9 August 1996," South African History Online, updated June 17, 2019, https://www.sahistory.org.za/archive/speech-president-nelson-mandela-womens-day-pretoria-9-august-1996.

Table *of* Contents

CHAPTER one

Let's be honest.
Shit's not working.

L et's start with the most important thing. This is the one thing I really want you to understand, so I'm going to say it first so that, even if you don't read the whole book, you get this. If you feel like you don't quite fit in, if you've ever had to change who you are, been told you're too much or not enough, doubted yourself, or wondered, "Is it me?" the truth is, if you are a woman or woman-identifying person, the world you're living in today was not built by or for you.

Let me say that again. *You're living in a world that wasn't built by or for you.*

What that means is there will be times when you feel like who you are and how the world is don't go together very well. It's not you. Those feelings of misalignment between your head and heart and the rest of the world are real, and, frankly, they are an appropriate response to what's going on out there. It's your senses and your intelligence telling you that something out there isn't adding up. It isn't. Feeling like you don't quite fit sometimes is just you being perceptive and smart, which you are. It still sucks, but there are reasons for it that have nothing to do with you. And we're going to explore those reasons in this book, as well as what to do about them.

A world that is equitable for women and men is better for us all. If common sense alone isn't enough to make the case for this, the research is irrefutable. Everything gets better when women and men participate and lead equally. And this will only happen if women and men work together to make it happen. We owe it to ourselves, each other and especially the next generations to do this work together today. My certainty in this has only grown the more I've read and researched and listened—to women, but also to men who are allies and feminists, and by feminist I simply mean those who believe that all genders should have equal rights and opportunities.

A word for and about men. Men, please read this book—not only to better understand the women in your life and what they are facing as they grow and evolve in a world that wasn't built for them and pushes back on them, but because the gender binary that is so deeply ingrained in our society creates a box for men too. It's a different box, yes, but for men who are trying to be whole and live sensitive, rich and emotional lives, it's a box that can do deep damage to men and boys too. But I will own that this book was written to speak directly to women. So, if you are a man reading this book, you will have to accept that you will be de-centred. You are not the leading character in this story. That can be unfamiliar and a bit challenging when the world has centred you in the story for so long, but I promise it's a worthwhile experience. You will grow.

Several years ago, I was approaching 50. Anyone who's ever gotten to that point can probably relate to the shock. *I am going to be 50? What happened? That's like, my grandmother or something.* But there it is. If we're lucky, we get to see 50, but that realization hit me like a ton of bricks anyway. If I was 50, that meant I was halfway done, because yeah, I planned to live to be 100. But what that milestone did was wake me up big-time. If I only had half of my life left, then I did not have unlimited time to have a positive impact on the world around me. This realization got me into action, but it wasn't a smooth transition. Like many of us, I needed to go through a crisis of consciousness first, before I could figure out what to do with the half of my life I had left. It was a messy, multi-year process of recognizing what I no longer wanted to do or be, of recognizing the places where I had turned away from social responsibilities in order to manage a business and raise a family and get dinners on the table every damn day and pay the bills, like all of us. That life stuff is consuming, and that's fair, but the gift of aging is that it asks you to decide—keep going like this, or do the next part differently?

When I was a kid, I used to say to myself, "I want to live an exceptional life." And what Brené Brown has taught us, among so many things, is that to do so we need to be vulnerable and brave and put ourselves out there. Step into the arena, as she says, and dare greatly.[1] Getting older holds up the mirror to that. Had I been living an exceptional life? Had I been daring greatly? I wasn't so sure. But as I passed the halfway point of my life, I knew in my heart I wanted to live that way more than anything. But how?

That story will unfold as we go. For now, let's get to the root of this book. If you look around the world and are worried, you are not alone. As Russia invades Ukraine, my gut twists. As the climate scientists tell us we are missing the critical targets we need to hit, it worries me deeply. And I look at that and wonder, *How in the hell can we solve for some of these issues that feel so global, so big?* The answer that I keep coming back to is that I believe we do not have the right leaders, the right decision-makers running this place. Are we making progress on many issues around the world? Yes. Is there less abject poverty, more clean water? Are there more girls getting educated, more women in leadership? Yes, absolutely. Kudos for all the amazing progress being made, but it's nowhere near enough.

We still don't have equal rights and opportunities for all. We still don't have representative diversity at the decision-making tables of the world. A small homogeneous group of some combination of white, straight, middle-aged-or-older, cis-gender men are making most of the decisions for the rest of us. And that's not working. If we had actual representative leadership at every decision-making table in our world, different, better decisions would get made. And the simple math for me was that, if women are just over 50% of the population, we should be running 50% of everything. Women should be 50% of every decision-making body, plain and simple. And it's

---

1   Brené Brown, *Daring Greatly: How the Courage to Be Vulnerable Transforms the Way We Live, Love, Parent, and Lead* (New York: Avery, 2012).

not just me who thinks that. The research on women participating in leadership and decision-making is clear: it makes things better in every way, and yet, we're nowhere close to 50% in pretty much every setting.[2]

The other thing that I knew to be true from my years of working with leadership teams around the world was that, when women did get into leadership roles, their experiences were very different from those of their male counterparts. Women, even in executive roles, were still being told to "be nice" and not advocate too hard, were still feeling that their voices didn't carry the same weight, were still being expected to do the team "housekeeping" work of note-taking or planning events and were still being subtly and not-so-subtly excluded, gaslit, shut down and held to very different performance standards and criteria for success. Many women, even once they arrive in leadership roles, still feel like they don't quite belong or like they have to fit into a world built for the men.[3]

These realizations sent me on a journey that would have me leave my successful leadership development consulting practice behind and create a new business, the Women's Leadership Intensive, with a mission to inspire, empower, support and equip women to lead the change the world needs—because of course, I couldn't change all this on my own, but I could support other women to step in and do that work in whatever industry or setting they were in. It's also what eventually pushed me to put what I've learned and heard and been

2   "10 Reasons Why the World Needs More Women in Leadership Roles," NaturalHR, March 23, 2021, https://www.naturalhr.com/2021/03/23/10-reasons-why-the-world-needs-more-women-in-leadership-roles/.

3   "5 Challenges That Female Leaders Face in the Workplace," Kelley School of Business, August 5, 2020, https://execed.kelley.iu.edu/5-challenges-that-female-leaders-face-in-the-workplace/.

thinking about into this book, even though I actively resisted doing so—because what business owner, woman, mother has time to write a book? Not me, but here I am. It needed to be said.

On this journey, I have struggled with the weight of inequalities in the world, with the complexity of the problems and the truth that there is no easy solution for any of them. The first half of this book will outline many of what I see as these problems. And yet, the more I learn, the more optimistic and motivated I become. If we can look these issues in the face, if we can start understanding them better, talking about them in new ways, and bringing more people to the table to address them, we will come up with better solutions, but the process will not be easy. Gloria Steinem said, "The truth will set you free, but first it will piss you off."[4] Yes to that. It's both. I am extremely pissed off about inequality, and some days it overwhelms me, and I just can't manage it. And yet, I have never felt so free. The freedom to speak about these issues from my own perspective and to hear the perspectives of others has been liberating and motivating. You may move back and forth between these experiences as you read this book—between pissed off and felling free. In the early chapters in particular, we'll work through a lot of problems, but we will get to optimism, too, because at my core I believe that if we actually work on these problems together, then we have a way better chance of solving them. In the end, I am honestly optimistic about the possibilities for a better future. But first, let's look at some of those weighty "truths."

I think back to one particular Friday. Fridays were my writing days,

---

4   Gloria Steinem, *The Truth Will Set You Free, But First It Will Piss You Off!: Thoughts on Life, Love, and Rebellion* (New York: Random House, 2019).

so I was writing. I got up to make a cup of coffee, and my partner shared with me a few choice tidbits from Twitter. He's a Twitter-er. I am not. I am reluctant on social media at best. My partner usually starts the day with a few scrolls before making school lunches as I silently sip my coffee and wait for my brain to (hopefully) fire up and come back to life.

The Twitter tidbit of that morning was that there was this 13-year-old kid playing hockey, and he happened to be Black. If you don't live in a place like Canada, where hockey is part of the national culture, you may not know that there are not a lot of Black hockey players out there. This young person was playing, and had been enduring some truly horrific racist taunts all season long. This is in 2019, and although this took place in the U.S., you can find similar stories in Canada too, a country where we like to think we're pretty progressive, not racist, and rather nice. Ultimately, P.K. Subban, a Toronto born, Black NHL hockey defenseman, publicly responded in support of this young man. And I'm glad he did. He used his voice and platform to address racism and support this young person. But my question is, Where the hell were the rest of us? Why in 2019 (and beyond) were the good people of any town or city not shutting that down, immediately and forcefully? Why weren't the perpetrators of hate and racism thrown out? Surely there must have been other people, and other white people in that arena who did not agree or condone what they were hearing. Where were they? Where were their voices and actions?

The real purpose of this book is a call to action to all of us good people to get going. Many of us have resources we may not know we have, like a voice, a sense of what's right, moral outrage or a desire for justice and equality. Each one of us getting into action is what will change the world. It's a paradox that these small, everyday things lead to big change, but there it is.

You've got to think about big things while you're doing small things, so that all the small things go in the right direction.

—ALVIN TOFFLER[5]

A conversation like the one about the hockey incident could happen in my household (and many households) any day of the week because events like this still happen every day of the week. We like to think about the progress we're making so we can tell ourselves that, as long as we're progressing, we'll be fine. But, my friends, that progress is nowhere near fast enough when you're the marginalized one, when you're the one being penalized by the system, when you're that 13-year-old kid on the ice. Slow change is fine if you're managing in the status quo, or even better if you benefit from it, if you personally are not experiencing micro- or macroaggressions, inequality, marginalization and exclusion. But if you experience any of that, you know that progress is just too slow, too little, too late. The problem is, the decisions are still overwhelmingly made by those who benefit from the systems and institutions as they are, so change continues to be slow and often performative.

On our current course, we may well be headed for a social and environmental crash. We're peeking out from between our fingers because we can see it coming. Many of us don't want to look too closely

---

5   "Memo to management," *Newsweek* 111, no. 10 (1988): 4–5.

because it scares the hell out of us. The systems and institutions that we've relied on forever don't work for everyone equally and haven't for a long time. We still have persistent and crippling inequalities, increasing income disparity, unresolved systemic racism and sexism, a global pandemic that disproportionately impacted women and people of low socioeconomic status, and an ongoing global gap between rich and poor countries. Not to mention a climate crisis that has finally been acknowledged but still largely ignored by world leaders because the change it demands is way beyond incremental or superficial.

Despite a growing awareness of inequalities, the numbers don't seem to be improving, and, in some cases, things are actually getting worse. There's the inevitable pushback that comes when change takes place, the one step forward, two steps back effect. Not sure about the pushback? Ask yourself how abortion rights got clawed back in the U.S. in 2021–2022 after years of advocacy, legal battles and progress on women's reproductive sovereignty. That's the kind of insidious pushback I'm talking about, the backwards effect where those with power clamp down on the rights of others in order to not only keep their power, but to actively disempower others. These displays of power are intended to scare us to the root of our beings—our physical bodies, our safety and security—and thereby to shut us up and shut us down.

We still have deep gender inequality everywhere in the world.

If you're a woman in North America, you are likely working very hard, especially if you also have caregiving responsibilities for children, parents, siblings or others in your community. Women make up 47% of the labour force in North America, according to the World

Bank. But women are still not making as much money for their efforts as their male counterparts; 82 cents on the dollar in the U.S., 89 cents in Canada. If you're a Black woman in the U.S., it's worse. You are paid 37% less than white men and 20% less than white women.[6] If you're an Indigenous woman in the U.S., it's even harder. You are paid 40% less than white men and 24% less than white women.[7] And as we know, women still carry a hugely disproportionate load of domestic, caregiving, emotional, social and other unpaid "invisible" labour. More to come on that—that's a whole chapter of its own.

Although women are almost half of the workforce, we collectively hold almost none of the leadership and highest-paid roles. Women make up 3.3% of CEOs of TSX-listed companies; we sit at around 30% on boards.[8] In politics, we're at 30.5% in Canadian Parliament[9] and 27% in the U.S. Congress—both the highest numbers ever, but nowhere near parity.[10] And if we break those numbers down, we still see that the biggest gaps exist at the top. In Canada, only 14 women have ever been first ministers (prime minister or premier) out of over

6   "Same Gap, Different Year," Institute for Women's Policy Research, September 2020, https://iwpr.org/wp-content/uploads/2020/09/Gender-Wage-Gap-Fact-Sheet-2.pdf.

7   Jasmine Tucker, "Equal Pay for Native Women," National Women's Law Center, September 2019, https://nwlc.org/wp-content/uploads/2018/11/Native-Women-Equal-Pay-2019.pdf.

8   "Women in the Workforce: Canada (Quick Take)," Catalyst, August 19, 2020, https://www.catalyst.org/research/women-in-the-workforce-canada/.

9   "Women in the Parliament of Canada: 100 Years of Representation," Library of Parliament, December 1, 2021, https://hillnotes.ca/2021/12/01/women-in-the-parliament-of-canada-100-years-of-representation/.

10   Carrie Blazina and Drew DeSilver, "A Record Number of Women Are Serving in the 117th Congress," Pew Research Center, January 15, 2021, https://www.pewresearch.org/fact-tank/2021/01/15/a-record-number-of-women-are-serving-in-the-117th-congress/.

300 in total.[11, 12] Canada did have a female prime minister once, the Right Honourable Kim Campbell. She became prime minister when Brian Mulroney resigned and was prime minister for only 132 days before losing the next election.[13] She sums it up well:

> People ask me, "Are you proud of the fact that you were Canada's first woman prime minister?" I respond, "Yes, but I'd be prouder still to say I was Canada's tenth woman prime minister."[14]

In general, when women do gain first minister positions, they don't last as long, don't get re-elected, suffer intense scrutiny and are subject to all manner of abuse.[15] Thank you social media for providing a new venue to abuse women with impunity and anonymity. The U.S. has never elected a woman president. The recent appointment of Kamala Harris as vice president has been the closest women, and women of colour, have ever come to seeing themselves in the highest leadership roles in the country.[16]

The real issue with gender inequality in leadership is the lack of diversity at decision-making tables, which is a root cause of the lack of

11 "List of Prime Ministers of Canada," Britannica, accessed May 5, 2022, https://www. britannica.com/topic/list-of-prime-ministers-of-Canada-1800352.

12 "Heather Stefanson Will Be Manitoba's First Female Premier," Canadian Crossing, October 31, 2021, https://balanceoffood.typepad.com/canadian_crossing/2021/10/heather-stefanson-will-be-manitobas-first-female-premier.html.

13 "Kim Campbell," No Second Chances, accessed April 30, 2022, https://nosecondchances.ca/firstministers/kim-campbell/.

14 "100 Years of Women and the Vote," Legislative Assembly of British Columbia, accessed April 30, 2022, https://www.leg.bc.ca/wotv/pages/featured-women/kim-campbell.aspx.

15 Elizabeth Renzetti, "Why Has Canada Had So Few Female First Ministers?" *The Globe and Mail*, April 27, 2019, https://www.theglobeandmail.com/opinion/article-why-has-canada-had-so-few-female-first-ministers/.

16 Lisa Lerer and Sydney Ember, "Kamala Harris Makes History as First Woman and Woman of Color as Vice President," *The New York Times,* November 7, 2020, https://www.nytimes.com/2020/11/07/us/politics/kamala-harris.html.

real systemic change happening. It's a rare person in the 1% who will advocate for giving up that power and privilege in order to distribute it more equitably in society. Most of those who hold that level of status and power make decisions that reinforce and perpetuate it.

Income disparity is getting worse, not better.

If we look at the overall economic outlook for most average folks, we see that economic policy clearly hasn't benefited everyone equally. We've all heard the phrase "the rich get richer." Well, it's true. In Canada, while the overall average income has risen, that average is mostly bumped up because the richest 1% got significantly richer, while the poorest income groups saw minimal increases.[17] According to Inequality.org, Americans "in the top 1% average over 39 times more income than the bottom 90%. But that gap pales in comparison to the divide between the nation's top 0.1% and everyone else. Americans at this lofty level are taking in over 196 times the income of the bottom 90%."[18]

The issue is not just the current income disparity, but that income inequality accumulates and deepens over generations. We hear stories of the self-made man, and yet behind most of those in the top 10%—and especially the 1%—what you'll find is resources, investment in education, networks and connections that most of us couldn't imagine. Never mind the inheritance of actual wealth that supports them to do things like start businesses or run for office.

Add a global pandemic to make things really interesting.

17   "Canadian Income Inequality," The Conference Board of Canada, accessed April 29, 2022, https://www.conferenceboard.ca/hcp/hot-topics/canInequality.aspx.
18   "Income Inequality in the United States," Inequality.org, accessed April 29, 2022, https://inequality.org/facts/income-inequality/.

The global pandemic that began in 2020 was not only a global health crisis, but it also revealed and heightened existing inequalities and took them to crisis level. The pandemic and its economic fallout are having a regressive effect on gender equality. According to the McKinsey & Company Report on Women in the Workplace 2020, women's jobs are 1.8 times more vulnerable to this crisis than men's jobs. Women make up 39% of global employment but account for 54% of overall job losses.[19] The study finds that the pandemic is "significantly increasing the burden of unpaid care, which is disproportionately carried by women," resulting in increased rates of burnout and decreased capacity to participate in the workforce.

Another McKinsey & Company study, this one in 2021, finds:

> Women are even more burned out than they were a year ago, and burnout is escalating much faster among women than among men. One in three women says that they have considered downshifting their career or leaving the workforce this year, compared with one in four who said this a few months into the pandemic. Additionally, four in ten women have considered leaving their company or switching jobs—and high employee turnover in recent months suggests that many of them are following through.[20]

In areas where COVID lockdowns took place, schools and day cares closed their doors and it was women, many of whom were in the

---

19   Anu Madgavkar et al. "COVID-19 and Gender Equality: Countering the Regressive Effects," McKinsey & Company, July 15, 2020, https://www.mckinsey.com/featured-insights/future-of-work/covid-19-and-gender-equality-countering-the-regressive-effects.

20   Tiffany Burns et al. "Women in the Workplace 2021," McKinsey & Company, September 27, 2021, https://www.mckinsey.com/featured-insights/diversity-and-inclusion/women-in-the-workplace.

throes of figuring out how to work remotely, keep jobs, or find new ones as their industries took a hit, who stepped up to manage children's education. It's always been a reality for working moms that they had two full-time roles, the first and second shifts, but day care and school buffered that for six to eight hours each day and made it just barely manageable. When those support systems disappeared, that precarious balance shattered, and many women were put in the impossible position of trying to work and raise and educate children at the same time. Never mind those who were also caring for parents, siblings or others.

Compounding the burden of childcare on women is the reality of the gender pay gap. Chances are that most women still earn less than their male partners do. So, in a pandemic, when someone has to look after children, it makes economic sense for that someone to be the woman in most heterosexual households. This doubled down on the expectation that women would step up at home and pull back at work.

But what about households where there is no male partner? That pay gap hits even harder, as does the impact of the pandemic. Many of the industries that were levelled by COVID-19 were female-dominated industries, already lower-paying jobs, and now disappeared altogether. Service industries, food services, retail, tourism, childcare, household labour—all low-paying jobs for women, and all hit hard by the pandemic.[21]

The temporary economic supports put in place helped some. But the

---

21   Nicole Bateman and Martha Ross, "Why Has COVID-19 Been Especially Harmful for Working Women?" Brookings, October 2020, https://www.brookings.edu/essay/why-has-covid-19-been-especially-harmful-for-working-women/.

recovery is still in progress, and people who went into debt to survive 2020 and 2021 are yet to have the next wave of reckoning. What will happen when those bills come due?

Why would we accept that, during a global crisis, some billionaires became mega billionaires, and some of the most disadvantaged in our society suffered and went deeper into debt and crisis?[22] Does the free-market economy justify that? Does it trump everything? Is it more important than looking after people? I don't think so. The research on Nordic countries, for example, shows that societies who take care of their most vulnerable are healthier and happier than those who do not.[23]

And while we're on the subject of the economy, we're still arguing that maintaining the current fossil fuel–based economic model is more important than accepting and dealing with the climate crisis, even though scientists are urgently imploring us to make more drastic, systemic changes, and fast. When are world leaders going to make the tough decisions about the climate crisis? And why aren't our current leaders making those decisions?

At the 2021 UN Climate Change Conference, the number one goal was to:

> Secure global net zero by mid-century and keep 1.5 degrees within reach.

22   Aimee Picchi, "Billionaires Got 54% Richer During Pandemic, Sparking Calls for Wealth Tax," CBS News, March 31, 2021, https://www.cbsnews.com/news/billionaire-wealth-covid-pandemic-12-trillion-jeff-bezos-wealth-tax/.

23   Zamira Rahim, "Norway Is Happiest Country in the World. What's the Secret?" *Time*, accessed April 30, 2022, https://time.com/collection/guide-to-happiness/4706590/scandinavia-world-happiness-report-nordics/.

Countries are being asked to come forward with ambitious 2030 emissions reductions targets that align with reaching net zero by the middle of the century.

To deliver on these stretch targets, countries will need to:

- ◉ Accelerate the phase-out of coal
- ◉ Curtail deforestation
- ◉ Speed up the switch to electric vehicles
- ◉ Encourage investment in renewables[24]

Phrases like *encourage, speed up* and *curtail* are suggestions with a lot of room for interpretation. While we're encouraged to switch to renewables, the Canadian government continues to push for oil pipelines,[25] the U.S. is the world's top oil producer, and Canada comes in at number four.[26] If the wealthy countries don't do more than "encourage" change, who will?

Young climate activists are calling for more concrete commitments that are in line with the recommendations of climate science, not politics. Greta Thunberg recently started using the phrase "blah, blah, blah" to describe her interpretation of the global political response to climate crisis.[27]

---

24   "COP26 Goals," UN Climate Change Conference UK 2021, accessed April 30, 2022, https://ukcop26.org/cop26-goals/.

25   Huileng Tan, "The Premier of Alberta Is Pushing for the Revival of the Trump-Backed Keystone XL Oil Pipeline to Replace Russian Imports to the US," Business Insider, March 8, 2022, https://www.businessinsider.com/keystone-oil-pipeline-alberta-premier-urges-revival-russia-ukraine-energy-2022-3.

26   "The World's Top Oil Producers," Investopedia, updated March 7, 2022, https://www.investopedia.com/investing/worlds-top-oil-producers.

27   Damian Carrington, "'Blah, Blah, Blah': Greta Thunberg Lambasts Leaders over Climate Crisis," *The Guardian*, September 28, 2021, https://www.theguardian.com/environment/2021/sep/28/blah-greta-thunberg-leaders-climate-crisis-co2-emissions.

According to a 2021 NPR article entitled "Young People Are Anxious About Climate Change and Say Governments Are Failing Them," the impact on the younger generations is devastating:

> For a forthcoming study, researchers with the U.K.'s University of Bath and other schools spoke to 10,000 people in 10 countries, all of whom were between the ages of 16 and 25, to gauge how they feel about climate change. The prevailing response could be summed up in two words: incredibly worried. And the respondents say governments aren't doing enough to combat climate change.
>
> ...Scientists say that nations aren't passing the right kinds of bold policies to avert the worst effects of climate change. The survey suggests that young people around the world grasp how widespread and dangerous political inaction is on climate change.
>
> The study concluded that there's a correlation between negative emotions, such as worry, and beliefs that government responses to climate change have been inadequate. So the way governments have been addressing—or failing to address—climate change is directly affecting the mental health of young people.[28]

Children feel less hopeful about the future than their parents. These young people have been raised in the information age. They understand the science, they believe it and they want a response from the people who hold the power and make the decisions. They are crying

---

28 Sharon Pruitt-Young, "Young People Are Anxious About Climate Change and Say Governments Are Failing Them," NPR, September 14, 2021, https://www.kuow.org/stories/young-people-are-anxious-about-climate-change-and-say-governments-are-failing-them.

for leaders to do something to protect their future. And they are being failed by the maintaining of the status quo, which continues to be the net response from many of our leaders. We continue to have fossil fuel economies, eat an animal-based diet in the rich West and not meet our targets even when we do agree to them. Bottom line is a lack of political will for bigger systemic change. Many decision-makers are putting their short-term wants ahead of the difficult decisions that would ensure long-term sustainability for the future. In the U.S., for example, members of congress who vote against the environment consistently gain greater campaign investments from big oil and gas:

> Results consistently support the investment hypothesis. In 13 out of 14 analyses, lower LCV scores (i.e., more antienvironmental votes) in one election cycle predicted significantly increased contributions in the following election cycle. For example, the strongest result was observed for the 2016 election: For every additional 10% of congressional votes against the environment in 2014, a legislator would receive an additional $5,400 in campaign contributions from oil and gas companies in 2016 (b = -0.54, SE = 0.12; P < 0.001; 95% CI [-0.77, -0.31]). This is an especially strong relationship considering that many elected officials vote against environmental policies nearly 100% of the time, thereby compounding the cycle of antienvironmentalism and increasing rewards in the form of contributions.[29]

To me, that means we have the wrong leaders. If these young peo-

---

29   Matthew Goldberg et al. "Oil and Gas Companies Invest in Legislators That Vote Against the Environment," *Environmental Sciences* 117, no. 10 (February 24, 2020): 5111–5112, https://doi.org/10.1073/pnas.1922175117.

ple were in office, what would be different? Why is it that we value the perspective of the middle-aged (white, cis) man more than anyone else's perspective? Why do we continue to appoint and elect and hire them into leadership roles to the exclusion of almost everyone else? Our actions suggest that we still believe these men are the only ones we trust to lead us—and yet the results are clear and consistent, showing that it's no longer working, if it ever did.

So, if you've been feeling scared and uncertain, you're on to something. It's not just you. And what got us here won't get us to somewhere better. It never has. We need new leadership and new leaders to solve these problems and take us into a new and better future. In the simplest terms, we need more women, and not just any women. We need women who are willing and able to lead, and lead as themselves, not by behaving like the men who have gone before them.

You might be asking yourself, "What about men? Can't men be part of this revolution too?" Of course they can. But they'll need to do the same thing I'm calling on women to do: question all the things we've been told are "just the way it is," connect with what they truly value, understand their own biases and assumptions, and be willing to take the risk to lead real change. The longer we ignore the realities of our current situation, the more damage gets done.

We need leaders who will act. Now.

Ellen Duffield suggests the kind of leadership we need today and for the future in her book *Brave Women: Building Bridges to Transformation, a Compendium*:

> The complexity, connectedness and challenges of our world require people who are willing to look beyond—beyond the

perspective of one culture or philosophy, beyond the problems to transformational process, beyond where we are to where we could be—and who are committed to building bridges across these chasms. Bridge Building Leaders. It turns out that many women are particularly skilled at this. However, for a whole variety of reasons, many women struggle with low confidence in leadership. This low confidence comes at a high price—personally, organizationally and globally. We need Bridge Building Leaders who are BRAVE. Brave, Resilient, Advocates, with Voice and Expanded Perspective.[30]

The good news is that women are gaining confidence every day, and so many people are waking up and demanding representation and equality that we can't ignore it anymore. The jig is up. The bad news is that every system in our society is still stacked against change. But we have what it takes to flip the scales. And this book will show you how.

---

30   Ellen Duffield, *BRAVE Women: Building Bridges to Transformation* (Connecticut: Shadow River Ink, 2018).

CHAPTER two

The road to change exists. We're just not walking it.

We know that diversity can sometimes be more uncomfortable because things are less familiar—but it gets the best results.

— MEGAN SMITH[31]

W hat is the road to change? Simply put, it's diversity. The world seems to be waking up to the idea of diversity, as though it's some kind of intellectual breakthrough to recognize diversity. Diversity is a fact, always has been a fact, and

---

31   Megan Smith, "'Passion, Adventure and Heroic Engineering'…and Talent Inclusion," Huffington Post, October 11, 2013, https://www.huffpost.com/entry/women-in-tech_b_4086332.

always will be a fact. Look around. This is not a breakthrough. It is, however, a beginning, the first cracks of breaking down a system that has intentionally and systematically excluded some groups of people and centred others. And, make no mistake, these oppressive and exclusive systems will not go quietly.

If diversity is simply a fact, then the problem lies firmly in our lack of inclusion and the resultant lack of equality and equity. We're at a point in history where we know we need to change, and so many of us want change, but we humans also resist change, we find all the reasons why change can't be done, we cling to the known because the unknown is scary. I'm not saying change is easy or simple. I know that as our systems and institutions change, we'll all be on a journey of learning and growth and making mistakes and figuring it out as we go. But the fact is, the complexity of diversity exists and acting as if it does not is not only untrue, it's dangerous. It means we exclude entire groups of people, which is fundamentally wrong, and we exclude their perspectives and ideas, which means we're missing out on innovation and new solutions to society's most pressing problems. We've gotten very comfortable with a certain kind of leader—usually male, white, middle-aged, educated, cisgender and straight. We have trusted these men even when the evidence has shown us we should not. Yes, there are a lot of really smart, values-based men who are doing a great job in their leadership roles, but the scales are tipped way too far in that direction.

Here's my outrageous suggestion: let's shoot for representation in leadership. If middle-aged white dudes are, say, 33% of the population in North America, then we should shoot to have only 33% of all leaders at every level of leadership be middle-aged white dudes. I like simple math, and I'm not sure it needs to be more complicated than that.

But with change comes resistance, and somehow there are all kinds of objections for why this couldn't possibly happen. There's the old argument that we can't find enough women and racialized people who are qualified for the jobs. Given the graduation rates from college and university programs, we're over that one. Then comes the argument that they don't have enough experience. Any young person looking for a job can tell you how ridiculous it is to need experience to get a job, but then nobody gives you the job, so you can't get the experience. This is a vicious cycle that keeps some people in and some people out. There's plenty of research in candidate selection in hiring that shows that when resumes are blind, meaning no names that would indicate race or gender, there is an increase in diverse hiring and a reduction in the biases that attribute more competence and capability to men, particularly white men.

Our overall approach to change so far has often been superficial. Preserve the status quo and move some pieces around. And always, always make people fit the system instead of changing the system to fit the people. We have failed to capture the promise of diversity. The different perspectives, new ideas, creativity and innovation. We have overwhelming research proving diversity leads to improvements across every indicator you can think of, including profit and productivity, ethics, inclusion, culture, decreased greenhouse gas emissions, increased access to health care and education, enduring peace agreements, absolutely everything. So why do our diversity and inclusion efforts and numbers continue to be so painfully inadequate and not representative?

In this book we'll particularly look at gender diversity because that's our focus, but that in itself doesn't solve the inclusion problem. We need an intersectional lens that takes into account our multiple identities. Kimberlé W. Crenshaw is "a pioneering scholar and writer on civil rights, critical race theory, Black feminist legal theory, and race, racism and the law. In addition to her position at Columbia Law School, she is a Distinguished Professor of Law at the University of California, Los Angeles."[32] She describes intersectionality this way:

> Intersectionality is a lens through which you can see where power comes and collides, where it interlocks and intersects. It's not simply that there's a race problem here, a gender problem here, and a class or LBGTQ problem there.[33]

According to Crenshaw's faculty profile, her "work has been foundational in critical race theory," and she coined the term intersectionality,[34] "to describe the double bind of simultaneous racial and gender prejudice. Her studies, writing, and activism have identified key issues in the perpetuation of inequality, including the 'school-to-prison pipeline' for African American children."[35]

When I first started the Women's Leadership Intensive, I interviewed many women about women in leadership, what it meant to them, and what their experiences were. One of the women I interviewed was doing her PhD in Black women's history, and she gifted me with a course correction in my thinking that I'm embarrassed to admit I simply hadn't had as a white feminist. She told me her perspective on women's leadership was that, as a white woman, I had the privilege of looking at gender first, as my primary identity, my first intersec-

---

32 "Kimberlé W. Crenshaw," Columbia Law School, accessed April 30, 2022, https://www.law.columbia.edu/faculty/kimberle-w-crenshaw.

33 Ibid.

34 Merrill Perlman, "The Origin of the Term 'Intersectionality,'" *Columbia Journalism Review*, October 23, 2018, https://www.cjr.org/language_corner/intersectionality.php.

35 "Kimberlé W. Crenshaw."

tional slice. But for her as a Black woman, her primary identity and intersection was race—that was the more impactful identity. Being a woman was second. We cannot underestimate the difference in experiences when we take into account multiple identities and inter-sectionalities. Just as, for me, being a woman has defined so much of my life experience, that same order of magnitude of definition applies to every intersection and identity we have. Race, gender, sexual orientation, class, education, geography, etc.—all of it matters.

We each live a different set of identities and intersections. And we tend to be less concerned with the places where we are part of the dominant group. North America being white-dominant,[36] my own whiteness meant I was free to focus on the place where I was part of a marginalized group, being a woman, because where we feel, live and experience the consequences of inequality is where the drive for change comes from. This is why the burden for change, the burden for creating equality, always seems to fall to those who don't have the power in the system, those in the nondominant group, those experiencing the pain of inequality. But we all need allies, and thankfully, more of us are getting educated and waking up to the experiences of others and our roles in those experiences That will make the journeys easier. Dr. Sarah Kaplan of the Institute for Gender and the Economy says, "Being an ally means stepping aside to create opportunities and standing in front to take the heat."[37] White people need to get educated and do the work to eradicate anti-Black racism. It's white

---

36   Jennifer Bratter and Ellen Whitehead, "Population Composition by Race and Ethnicity: North America," *International Encyclopedia of the Social & Behavioral Sciences* (2015): 553–558, https://doi.org/10.1016/B978-0-08-097086-8.31118-7.

37   (((Dr. Sarah Kaplan))) (she/hers) (@sarah_kaplan), "Seems like a good day to repost this one: being an ally means stepping aside to create opportunities and standing in front to take the heat." Twitter, October 12, 2020, 2:39 PM, https://twitter.com/sarah_kaplan/status/1315723893437607936.

people who benefit from that system, regardless of whether we participated in creating it or not, and it's white people who hold so many positions of power and voice today. Similarly, men need to get educated and do the work of gender equality for the same reasons. Those with the power and privilege need to share.

I don't know that we have ignited the powers of the world to be able to make change. I almost see change as two levels, one kind of coming from the top and the other, it's like the grass root—let's make the change we want to see. But for both of them to work, people need to recognize the problem, they need to understand that a change will impact them, and essentially they're going to have to share. And I don't know if the desire to share is there, when there are clear benefits to staying in power.

—JAMILE CRUZ, *Founder & CEO, I&D 101*[38]

To think about your own intersectionality, have a look at the diagram below and ask yourself, "On each dimension, am I part of the privileged or powerful group? Or am I part of the marginalized or excluded group?" It's not about judging what you discover about your own identities, but rather understanding how many dimensions exist and how different identities lead to very different experiences of the world. We cannot assume that our own experience is representative of anyone else's. That's the beautiful complexity of diversity.

There were two profound learnings that grew from that seed of a conversation way back then. The first is that I need to work hard-

---

38   Interview with author, March 9, 2022.

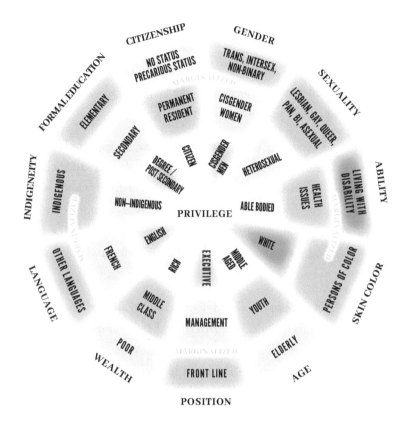

ADAPTED FROM CCRWEB.CA

er to consider differences in identity, especially in the places where I'm part of the privileged group—being white, educated, middle class, English-speaking, etc. Just like I get deeply frustrated when I'm talking with a man who doesn't understand the inequities I face every day as a woman, I imagine racialized and Indigenous people, LGBTQIA2S+ folks and members of other marginalized groups have been frustrated with me and my perspective, or lack thereof.

A word about the term *racialized*. Racial compared to whom? White people. Meaning white people are once again centred. How about

BIPOC? It groups together Black, Indigenous and other people of colour, who have very different histories and experiences in places like Canada or the U.S. So, what is the better way to have this conversation about race? I don't know—the language all feels problematic. I asked Jamile Cruz what she thought:

> It's understanding that when we use these terms, people of colour, BIPOC, we are trying to group people and say, there's a shared experience here that's only different from white, when it's not the case. Not being white creates an identity that has a lot more definitions throughout your experiences. The language and the grouping are problematic today, and it will continue to be problematic.
>
> The level of oppression and discrimination are not equal to all groups, intersectionality matters, and it is complex when we put everyone under the same umbrella. When using BIPOC, for example, we group Black and Indigenous people with other races. Asian people's experiences can be very different from Black people's experiences and Indigenous people's experiences. So yes, we're all not white, but we're not all the same.

The second big aha was that all marginalized groups do share some common ground, and we need to be careful not to be divided too deeply based on our differences. If we are for equality, we must be for equality for everyone. As a white feminist, I am clear that gender equity does not mean more privileged, white, wealthy women in leadership roles. And that's the way we're headed, by the way. That would be progress, but only along one axis. And that is not only morally wrong and unfair, it won't deliver on the promise of diversity. It doesn't bring enough difference of perspective and experience to the table. It only opens the door a small crack to a small number of women who already have more power and voice than others.

We also need to talk about the distinction between equality and equity. Equality is everyone getting the same thing. Think about it as everyone needs to get from point A to point B, so everyone gets a bike, the same bike—that would be equality, everyone gets the same thing. Right now, we don't have equality along any axis in our society. There have been estimates made about how long it would take to achieve gender equality at our current rate, and the numbers aren't looking good. At this pace, our daughters, granddaughters and great-granddaughters will face most of the same inequality that we have. If that isn't a wake-up call, I don't know what is. From the Bill & Melinda Gates Foundation:

> As we celebrate International Women's Day, let's pause to appreciate the progress we are making towards gender equality. In 46 countries, women now hold more than 30 percent of the seats in at least one chamber of the national parliament. Child marriage is on the decline worldwide and in Ethiopia, dropped by a third in the past decade. More women than ever before have access to family planning and in Uganda, the number of women using modern contraception nearly doubled (from 1.6 million in 2012 to 3.1 million in 2019).

> This progress is changing the course of hundreds of millions of lives and history. And yet, it is not enough. No matter your age, we will not achieve gender parity in your lifetime. Nor we will likely achieve it in your daughter's lifetime.

> We are on a trajectory that will have our granddaughters and great-granddaughters raising the victory flag for gender equality.

About 99 years from now.

This means generations more women and girls who cannot determine if, when, and whom they marry. It means generations more women and girls who cannot stay in school to achieve their ambitions. It means generations more women and girls who have no control over household finances to support their children's good nutrition, health, and education.

It also means generations of untapped potential and talent—potential and talent the world could use to help tackle big challenges, from combatting epidemics like COVID-19 to building new climate solutions.

We don't want to wait. And we know neither do you.[39]

So, equality is everyone getting the same bike to get where they need to go. Sounds good, right? Problem solved. Not so fast. Some people are bigger than others, some are smaller, some don't know how to ride a bike or have never had one before, some are really intimidated by bikes in general, some people have disabilities and a bike wouldn't work for them. What about all of those people? How does a bike help them? The answer is that it doesn't. Or at least, it doesn't help everyone equally. The issue is that equality assumes universality. It assumes we all need or want the same things and that as long as we can all get the same things, we're good. But we don't, and we aren't.

Sometimes I get questions about why we need a Women's Leadership Intensive. Why can't we just have a Human's Leadership Intensive? I

39   "We Don't Want to Wait 99 Years for Gender Equality," Bill & Melinda Gates Foundation, accessed April 30, 2022, https://www.gatesfoundation.org/ideas/articles/we-dont-want-to-wait-99-years-for-gender-equality.

get it, and I wish we were at a point where we don't need women-only spaces. But the truth is that we are not there. Women do need different leadership development opportunities because our leadership journeys have been very different than men's, because we still face barriers that our male colleagues do not, and we are very familiar with having our experiences and perspectives dismissed, minimized and discouraged in mixed-gender settings. We need a place where we are not trying to ride a bike that wasn't designed to fit us, because that's exhausting. We need spaces where our experiences are centred and recognized.

There is no one size fits all. When we try to create one, we base it on some kind of universal norm. Guess who has been the universal norm throughout history? You got it: men. "Average" white men. The world of work was built by and for them. Your car, the medicine you take, and pretty much every tool and object and system in our society were built for them. Not convinced? There's some fascinating research by women like Caroline Criado Perez and Katrine Marçal documenting how our world is designed by and for men, and what some of the consequences of that are. More from Marçal in the next chapter, but here's an example from Criado Perez's landmark book *Invisible Women: Data Bias in a World Designed for Men*:

> Men are more likely than women to be involved in a car crash, which means they dominate the numbers of those seriously injured in car accidents. But when a woman is involved in a car crash, she is 47% more likely to be seriously injured than a man, and 71% more likely to be moderately injured, even when researchers control for factors such as height, weight, seat-belt usage, and crash intensity. She is also 17% more likely to die. And it's all to do with how the car is designed—and for whom.

Crash-test dummies were first introduced in the 1950s, and for decades were based around the 50th-percentile male. The most commonly used dummy is 1.77 m tall and weighs 76 kg (significantly taller and heavier than an average woman); the dummy also has male muscle-mass proportions and a male spinal column. In the early 1980s, researchers...argued for the inclusion of a 50th-percentile female in regulatory tests, but this advice was ignored by manufacturers and regulators. It wasn't until 2011 that the US started using a female crash-test dummy—although, as we'll see, just how "female" these dummies are is questionable.[40]

Criado Perez goes on to describe how these "female" dummies are still not used in the majority of testing, are generally only used in the passenger seat when they are used, and are in fact scaled-down male dummies. We can say with confidence at this point that women are not simply smaller men. This is just one of many examples of how basing our world on the "male default" as a universal norm is problematic and has consequences, both large and small—as large as women being 17% more likely to die in car crashes, or taking medications that were not tested on women, and as small as finding the daily tools of living such as our smartphones are too big for our hands. We adapt, and we get so used to adapting that we don't even notice we're doing it anymore. Talk to any left-handed person about life designed for a right-handed world (scissors, anyone?), and you'll get a taste of the compensations made every day.

The male default or norm has been largely invisible, running in the

---

40   Caroline Criado Perez, *Invisible Women: Data Bias in a World Designed for Men* (New York: Abrams Press, 2019).

background of all our lives unconsciously. We know certain things don't fit us, but we thought that maybe that was just us. Nope. Things don't fit because they weren't designed by or for us. I just bought a new (well, used, but new to me) car. I can't reach the turn signal without removing my hand from the steering wheel. Why? Because I have woman-sized hands and cars are designed for men. That's a tiny example of how problematic the idea of universality can be. It will catch us in pretty much every dimension of our lives.

Even so, equality would be a more-than-welcome goal. It would be huge progress. But it still wouldn't fit for so many of us. It's equity that fundamentally includes the idea of diversity. Equity recognizes we are all different, and we come from different starting points. We don't all need a bike. Some of us might need a bike, but a bigger or smaller one. Some of us need a wheelchair. Some need a scooter or a car or a bus in order to get from A to B. That makes things way more complicated, but that's the reality. Diversity has inherent complexity, and if we can't deal with complexity, we'll never achieve equity. It requires us to consider, to listen, and to develop different solutions and options for different people.

So far, we've called this *accommodation*. That word is problematic in itself; it still implies a universal norm, and that those who don't conform to that norm require "special treatment," and it also makes it sound as if accommodation is optional (unless legislated). That's a fundamentally flawed notion for many reasons. First, it's inaccurate. The idea of the universal norm is simply the repeated playing out of those in power recreating the same systems, institutions and tools that reinforce their group's centred-ness or dominance. The dominant group has set the norms or defaults in their image. That image represents a very small percentage of humanity.

That centring of the dominant group means the rest of us need to fit in (and many of us have felt like we don't, or don't want to) or fight for accommodation. This keeps the power in the hands of the dominant, yet again. The company you work for can choose to accommodate your different ability, your caregiving responsibilities, your need for flexibility, or the fact that your voice is actively discouraged in meetings. Or your company can ignore those differences and require you to conform to the norm to fit in and keep your job, all the while calling it a policy of equality—"everyone here gets the same treatment"—which doesn't acknowledge the reality of different needs. The power differential persists, and it's painful.

If we assumed instead that diversity was the norm, *because it is*, how would we approach things differently? We wouldn't assume or expect that everyone wants or needs the same things. We wouldn't expect that the same things would work for everyone when we know that our experiences as women or people of colour or Indigenous people or LGBTQIA2S+ people are very different. If we assume diversity is the norm, then we accept the reality that people are complex, that there is no "norm," and we have a better chance of moving toward equity.

I'm a glass-half-full person, and here's what brings me hope. There is a path to solving some of our biggest social and environmental problems, and it's diversity, inclusion and equity. We've only been accessing a very small subset of the human potential to run this place. It's like we've been cooking a stew with only one ingredient and expecting to get a lot of exciting and different meal options out of it. If we were to access the diversity of perspectives and ideas that exist, we'd come up with better solutions. If we included more diverse people and perspectives in the leadership roles that shape policy, make decisions, steward our resources and create culture, we would get different solutions, values and outcomes. We would choose social and environmental policies that address some of the biggest challenges of our time, like racism, income disparity, climate crisis and war.

The issue is, we're not doing it. The same demographic of leaders continues to hold almost all the decision-making power in the world. We're not accessing diversity and we still lack inclusion and equity. The institutions of our society, and those who thrive in them, keep reinforcing the status quo because the status quo benefits them. This can be conscious or unconscious, but either way, it influences the decisions that get made. One of the most immutable arguments for why we can't change has been protecting the economy, the idea that we can't possibly change, especially not quickly, because we must preserve the economy. Fossil fuel economies and the climate crisis are a great example of this. We're killing the planet, but we'll continue to do so because, you know, the economy. As you may guess, our economic models are also based on selective data and particular perspectives. The economy is not some magical "truth" that must be upheld. It's a construct, and constructs can change.

CHAPTER three

We can't keep using the economy as an excuse for bad decisions.

In the later nineteenth and early twentieth centuries, women joined together to demand the right of inheritance, the right of ownership, the right to start their own companies, the right to borrow money, the right to employment, equal pay for equal work and the option to support themselves so that they didn't need to marry for money and could instead marry for love.

Feminism continues to be about money.

— KATRINE MARÇAL, *Who Cooked Adam Smith's Dinner?*[41]

---

41   Katrine Marçal, *Who Cooked Adam Smith's Dinner?: A Story of Women and Economics* (New York: Pegasus Books, 2017).

The argument that we need to protect the economy is one of our favourite and most flawed excuses for maintaining the status quo and doubling down on bad decisions. Even if you believe that the economy is the most important factor in our maintaining our civilization, the underpinnings of economic theory were created by humans, and guess what? Once again, those humans were men, men with resources and a particular perspective about the way the world works and the kinds of things that count as valuable, especially economically valuable.

It's getting worse over time. The system privileges the privileged and gets worse every year. And now it's just off the charts. It's gone exponential. Five people with the same wealth as half the planet. Getting worse and worse. It's working as it's designed and it's not equitable. We can do better. About 400 years ago we followed this path of individual self-interest over the collective. And, I mean, that was a fork in the road. We followed a philosophy and it's time to change it again.

—VICKY SAUNDERS,
Founder of SheEO, Serial Entrepreneur, Award-Winning Mentor [42]

Just as Indigenous peoples, racialized people and women have been asking why we should revere and never question the laws and rules that we had no hand in creating, I'd ask the same question about the economy. Because clearly, the current economic models work very well for some people, and not for others.

---

42   Interview with author, February 8, 2022.

For starters, economic models only count certain kinds of work. There are so many critical foundations of the economy that never get counted, namely caregiving work and domestic labour. Entire sectors of gendered labour have been undervalued or excluded altogether. Among many things the COVID pandemic has taught us is the reality that caregiving work is critical to the functioning of society. It always has been, but it has been conveniently invisible because most of it happened in the lives and work of women. During lockdowns around the world, the instant absence of day cares and schools meant that many, mostly women, either had to downshift their participation in the workforce or leave it altogether. And many of the sectors most impacted by lockdowns and restrictions were female-dominated, such as food service, retail, hospitality, caregiving, and domestic work, which meant that in addition to losing childcare and other care supports, many women lost jobs or were furloughed.

The idea that work-life and home-life are somehow separate was popularized in eras past and was based on the notion that men went to work while women stayed home. It was a clear-cut separation. Although that separation never existed for many women, and it's even less common today, there has been a persistent clinging to the idea that we draw a hard line between work and life.[43] In many settings, it is still considered unprofessional to have your home life impact your job in any way. Both men and women are expected to work as if they don't have a home, a family, caregiving responsibilities, day-care drop-offs, or sick kids to pick up from school in the middle of any given Wednesday afternoon.

---

43   "Defining Work-Life Balance: Energy Is the Missing Ingredient," Kumanu, accessed April 30, 2022, https://www.kumanu.com/defining-work-life-balance-its-history-and-future/.

For a long time, we pulled this off, because we had to. We were able to maintain the illusion of separation between home and work because women juggled home responsibilities on lunch hours and after work and relied on services like day care and school to care for and educate children while they participated in the workforce. But the balance was always tenuous. Families who worked low-paying jobs couldn't afford day care, and even those who had it could get the call at any moment that a child was sick and needed to go home. The demands of the workday never mapped to the availability of care. If a workday is at minimum 9:00 to 5:00, but schools run from 9:00 to 3:00, then how do we make that work, taking into account commutes, bus schedules and all the other pieces of the puzzle?

We live in a rural area, so, when my son Gabe was little, he would get on the school bus at 8:00 and off again at 4:00. We were lucky because that bus time gave my partner just enough time to drop Gabe at the bus and get to work by 8:30. As a teacher, my partner could race out the door at 3:30 to meet the bus again at the end of the day. But one traffic jam, one conversation at work on the way out the door, would make the whole thing fall apart. And like so many women, my male partner experienced what it's like to be judged during those years as somehow not as committed to his job because he didn't stay late at school like many of his colleagues could. He had many conversations about how, no, his wife could not be doing all this childcare work. My job has always involved travel but if it did not, the default assumption at work would have been that drop offs and pick ups would be my responsibility, not his.

I share this as an example of a really fortunate scenario because it was workable, and because it wasn't all on me. That's not true for many families, making before- and after-school programs or cobbling together childcare with friends and relatives part of the daily juggling that mostly women do just to show up to work, let alone to perform and progress at their jobs. When COVID caused all of that to go up in a puff of smoke, the cracks in the system became canyons and many women fell through. The truth is that there never was a hard separation between work and home for women. We just got really good at making it look that way because it was a demand of the job, and of workplace culture in general.

And what about other care work? The pandemic showed us clearly that we've taken that work for granted and, in many jurisdictions, have cut and cut away at funding and infrastructure. Even in Canada, where we have tax-funded universal health care, we continued to undervalue female-dominated health-care professions during the pandemic itself. The rates of pay for full-time registered nurses start at around $33.23 per hour, reaching as high as $47.57 per hour, according to the Ontario Nurses' Association (ONA).[44] In 2020, Ontario nurses received a 1% pay increase[45] (while inflation was 3.4%)[46] in the middle of a global pandemic that had them working around the clock in unbearable conditions. The Ontario conservative government introduced Bill 124 to limit salary increases for public sector workers like nurses and teachers (female-dominated fields) while exempting paramedics, firefighters and police (male-dominated fields) from the same limits. How is that not a gendered pay gap? Nurses rightly referred to the move as a "slap in the face" and called

---

44 Lisa Xing, "1% Pay Increase Under Public-Sector Wage Cap a 'Slap in the Face,'" Ontario Registered Nurses Say," CBC News, June 11, 2020, https://www.cbc.ca/news/canada/toronto/ontario-nurses-pay-increase-ona-covid-doug-ford-1.5607068.

45 Ibid.

46 Jordan Press, "Canada's Annual Inflation Rate Hits 3.4%, Highest Level in Nearly a Decade," Global News, May 19, 2021, https://globalnews.ca/news/7875430/inflation-canada-statisitcs-canada/.

it out as gendered. While being hailed as heroes, they were being undercut, underpaid and undervalued.[47]

Economics, like most systems and institutions in our society, was invented by humans, in particular men of a certain social class. They saw the world in a very particular way, and that way doesn't fit for many of us. Our economic systems have failed to include and to allow for mobility between socioeconomic status groups. The economy protects those who are winning at it. Everyone else works to scaffold it. Theories like "trickle-down economics" have become government policy and persist despite their obvious failure and general lack of common sense:

> Trickle-down economics is a theory that claims benefits for the wealthy trickle down to everyone else. These benefits are tax cuts on businesses, high-income earners, capital gains, and dividends.
>
> Trickle-down economics assumes that investors, savers, and company owners are the real drivers of growth. It promises they'll use any extra cash from tax cuts to expand businesses. Investors will buy more companies or stocks. Banks will increase lending. Owners will invest in their operations and hire workers. All of this expansion will trickle down to workers. They will spend their wages to drive demand and economic growth.
>
> ...The International Monetary Fund (IMF) also rejects the trickle-down theory. In its report authored by five economists, it argues that "...increasing the income share of the poor and the middle class actually increases growth while a rising income

---

47   Lisa Xing, "1% Pay Increase Under Public-Sector Wage Cap a 'Slap in the Face.'"

share of the top 20% results in lower growth—that is, when the rich get richer, benefits do not trickle down." The IMF's fight against income inequality revolves around the fact that expenditures of middle-to-low-income sectors are the drivers of the economy. Even a mere 1% increase in wealth for 20% of low-income earners yields a 0.38% growth in gross domestic product (GDP). On the other hand, increasing the income of the top 20% high-income earners results in a 0.08% *decrease* in GDP.[48]

Economic gaps not only persist over lifetimes and generations, but they compound. We know women make $0.89 for every dollar a man makes in Canada,[49] $0.82 in the U.S.[50] Here's how the gender pay gap compounds over the working life of a woman. It begins with our first jobs. Girl Guides of Canada partnered with Ipsos in 2018 to ask teens, ages 12 to 18, about their summer employment and revealed that girls face pay gaps and many other gender inequities on the job.[51]

According to the study, "in full-time summer jobs, girls earned about $3.00 per hour less than boys. The gap widened to $6.31 per hour for girls who worked in an informal setting for family, friends or

48 Kimberly Amadeo, "Why Trickle-Down Economics Works in Theory but Not in Fact," The Balance, December 30, 2021, https://www.thebalance.com/trickle-down-economics-theory-effect-does-it-work-3305572.

49 "The Facts About the Gender Pay Gap," Canadian Women's Foundation, updated March 15, 2022, https://canadianwomen.org/the-facts/the-gender-pay-gap/.

50 Janelle Jones, "5 Facts About the State of the Gender Pay Gap," U.S. Department of Labor Blog, March 19, 2021, https://blog.dol.gov/2021/03/19/5-facts-about-the-state-of-the-gender-pay-gap.

51 "Gender Wage Gap Occurring Among Youth Too; Canadian Girls on Average Making $3 Less Per Hour," Ipsos & Girl Guides of Canada, May 2019, https://www.ipsos.com/en-ca/news-polls/Canadian-Girls-Spent-Summer-2018-Working-Interning-Volunteering.

neighbours on a full-time basis—an area where girls are more likely to be employed relative to boys." Girls were also way more likely to be employed in jobs related to caring, food and beverage, and retail.[52] These are historically feminized and therefore low-paying jobs, with fewer opportunities for full-time work. So, it's not just about the fact that women and girls are not getting equal pay for equal work. In many cases, we don't have equal work. Women are streamed from those very first jobs into lower-paid, more precarious sectors, like the caregiving and service sectors. Sound familiar? Here's one woman's example. She told this story in one of our women's leadership programs, and it illustrates both the streaming of women into caregiving and lower-paying work and the difference in how we value and pay for those jobs versus the jobs that boys are streamed into:

> I always had a job growing up. I think one of my first jobs (other than babysitting) was in retail when I was in grade seven. Pretty sure it was because the owner of the store was a friend of the family.

> I do remember applying for jobs with "the city." This is where the good jobs were—they typically rehired every summer and paid well. I can't remember if I applied to a variety of departments within the city, but I do know that I was excited to interview for, and finally get, a job in Parks and Recreation as playground supervisor.

> My job entailed looking after, and entertaining, children of all ages every day, all day. Children were dropped off at the play-

---

52 "Girls on the Job: Realities in Canada," Girl Guides, April 2019, https://www.girlguides.ca/WEB/Documents/GGC/media/thought-leadership/girlsonjob/GirlsOnTheJobRealitiesInCanada.pdf.

ground, and the expectation was that I kept them safe and provided engaging activities and experiences for them throughout the entire day.

I remember the maintenance trucks that came by the playgrounds each week to do things like collect the garbage or cut the lawn. I would see some of the guys I went to high school with. I remember comparing notes one day—not sure how we got on the topic—but I do recall being quite miffed that they were getting paid a lot more than I was—not sure if it was double? But it was substantial. And I kept thinking, I was chasing high-energy kids all day and responsible for their safety and well-being, and the guys were driving around town, emptying garbage cans and cutting lawns—not that there is anything wrong with that. But even if that was equally as challenging or important, why the difference in wages? Even at that young age, something just felt wrong about it.

And there you have it. Why do we value some jobs more than others? Because they are jobs historically done by men, and we pay men more. It was never fair to pay women less or to stream women into low-paying careers, but it began at a time when men were considered "providers" and, as such, got paid more. That's not the reality anymore, and yet the inequity persists.

Let's dig deeper into the pay gap and how it compounds. Let's say you've got two college graduates, one man and one woman, interviewing for their first jobs at a medium-sized corporation. Most jobs of that nature have salary bands, a range of pay for any given job, usually based on criteria like experience, education, etc. Now we know there are conscious and unconscious biases that credit men with more competence and capability than women. Combine that with our history of paying men more and consider that men are often socialized to compete for rewards, ask for what they want and expect that it will be given, while women are socialized that it is unsightly to demand financial rewards and impolite to want too much and that they should be grateful for what they get.[53] Those factors compound, and we find that the male graduate asks for and is offered wages at the higher end of the pay range, while the female graduate asks for and is offered the low end.

We know that this isn't just a hypothetical because the pay gap is well-documented at every level and in every sector. We know that girls are conditioned from our very first jobs to expect less, and boys are conditioned to expect more. No surprises. There's your early career pay gap. You've got two candidates, and all other things being equal, you don't have equal pay for equal work.

The gap starts to compound when it's time to get a raise. Many pay raises are a percentage of current salary. So, if our two young people are doing the same job but the man is getting, say, $50,000 and the woman is getting $45,000, even if they both get the same percentage pay increase, the pay gap is going to not only persist but increase. For ease of numbers, let's say they both get a whopping 10% increase. Our man will get $5,000 and our woman $4,500. This means his salary just increased to $55,000 and hers to $49,500. So, what started in the first year on the job as a $5,000 pay gap just widened to $5,500. And so on and so on.

53   Joanne Lipman, "Women Are Still Not Asking for Pay Rises. Here's Why." WeForum, April 12, 2018, https://www.weforum.org/agenda/2018/04/women-are-still-not-asking-for-pay-rises-here-s-why/.

Even if both of our young people did start with the same salary and received the same increases the "motherhood penalty" will slow down many women's earning potential. Motherhood penalties are the gaps in career and earnings women experience for having children and taking parental leaves, which temporarily removes them from pay increases and promotion opportunities. Beyond the actual time away, women's potential childcare responsibilities have long been used as a reason why they are excluded from certain roles and positions. These same penalties have not been applied to men who are parents, and it will be interesting to see what changes as more and more men take parental leaves and choose to be more involved in the day-to-day activities of parenting, which by default shift focus away from work. This all runs within the backdrop of the overall gender gap in pay, promotions and access to higher paying jobs. This continues until such time as we get to the end of a woman's career, when we find that women retire with 80% the retirement funds of their male colleagues.[54]

This is a big problem for many reasons, one of which is that women live longer than men, so retirement income is even more critical to not just individual women, but to society as a whole. We know that elder poverty is more prevalent for women,[55] which, in turn, means a greater need for social service support. When we don't look after people in our society, it's not only unfair and cruel, it costs us in the end.

Even our government policies on retirement are gendered. Nancy

54   Christian Weller, Joelle Saad-Lessler, and Tyler Bond, "Still Shortchanged: An Update on Women's Retirement Preparedness," National Institute on Retirement Security, May 2020, https://www.nirsonline.org/reports/stillshortchanged/.
55   "Why Women Are More Likely Than Men to Face Poverty After Retirement," CBS News, July 11, 2016, https://www.cbsnews.com/news/women-more-likely-than-men-to-face-poverty-after-retirement/.

Wilson, an accountant and the CEO of the Canadian Women's Chamber of Commerce, describes the gendered Canadian RRSP system like this:

> There was certainly legislation that I knew of through my accounting training that was massively prejudicial against women. Or at least, if you want to flip it, it was massively advantageous to men. A great example is the RRSP legislation, the whole way that RRSPs are designed, and the calculation for RRSPs, it gives men a massive benefit in terms of accumulated tax-sheltered savings for retirement. Like mat leave benefits are not deemed earned income for RRSP purposes. Although you have to pay tax on them, they don't contribute to your contribution room in your RRSPs. So every time [a woman takes] a mat leave, and the man who made the baby is still earning and bulking up his contribution room, the woman, even though she's earning mat leave and that mat leave could be part of her contribution room, she's getting zero for those years or that period of time, even though she's paying tax on it.
>
> And men make more money, so that calculation for contribution room is always going to be bigger. The fact that they actually have more money to exploit that contribution room is bigger. And women live longer. So all of it is really, really...It's a sexist legislation, like it really is written for a man's career and a man's life.

We've been talking specifically about the gender pay gap and the implications of that. But there are many other groups facing similar and, in some cases, even greater gaps. And those gaps not only compound over a lifetime but result in generational poverty or generational wealth, depending on which side of the equation you're on. We often attribute wealth with work ethic, but if you've had a history of wealth or poverty then you are more likely to continue on that very same trajectory. And how many of us question where that original wealth came from? Many white people can trace our cultural and even ancestral roots back to colonialism and slavery.

Although there are various reasons why some groups have less wealth than others, if you have or earn less, you save less. If you save less, you have less to invest in your own education and career development, and you continue to earn less. You also have less to invest in the education and career development of your children, so they earn less. You have fewer assets to share or pass on to your children. There is no inheritance, no trust fund. There are no wealthy friends and colleagues to introduce to your children to help them get an opportunity, a good job, a better-paid job.

The way the North American economy is set up, wealth compounds over a lifetime and from generation to generation. And poverty does too. Yes, we hear stories of the great falling from wealth due to bad investments or poor judgments. And yes, we hear stories of the disadvantaged individuals who, despite all odds, make it to the "top." But those stories are the exceptions. For every disadvantaged individual who makes it through a system designed to shut them out and keep them out, there are a vast majority who cannot. They are working just as hard, and they are just as talented, smart, committed, caring. But they cannot beat a system that wasn't set up for them to win.

The other issue with these stories of the ones who "make it" is that they are held up as somehow different or better than others of their group. We see that one particularly hardworking woman can be the

CEO of her company, but most women cannot, even though they may work just as hard. That one exceptionally well-educated Black man sits among the white partners at his law firm, while most Black men cannot. The myth of the special individual does us no favours. It reinforces the belief that anyone who is not part of the dominant group *must* be special or exceptional in order to make it. What about the rest of us who are not? Who are great at what we do, intelligent, hardworking, regular people? Do we not deserve to participate? To be equal?

And why have we continued to excuse, promote and elect average white men? Why do we accept that average—and, in some cases, incompetent and flat-out selfish or stupid—white men can and should still succeed? Not only succeed, but run this place, run all the institutions and make all the decisions for the rest of us? If we are ever to have equality, we must at least be held to the same standards, and we are not. Those of us in nondominant groups are expected to be exceptional and above reproach. If we have the audacity to be imperfect or make a mistake, that just confirms that our group doesn't deserve to be there. "See, I told you a woman couldn't make it as president!" If we are to achieve equity, we must go further to create equal opportunities for success based on a variety of starting points. We won't get there if we expect those starting way behind on access to education, resources, networks and funds to not only play by the same rules as those who have way more advantages, but to be held to even higher standards. And that is what we expect today.

We've also put a lot of emphasis on equal pay for equal work, but we do not have equal work. Women hold 8.5% of the highest-paid positions in Canada's top 100 listed companies, according to a report by global executive search firm Rosenzweig & Company.[56] What that means is that the biggest decisions that get made by those at the top largely exclude women—decisions about supply chain, investment, environmental and sustainability practices, hiring, strategy, etc. Decisions that we may not think about but that have a huge impact on our day-to-day lives, on our society and economy.

Years ago, I was working on a global leadership development program, and it was having a huge impact in improving that organization's culture, leadership, productivity and safety. We had worked on values, diversity, team leadership and many other important topics. The internal team working on the project was truly transforming and facilitating that same transformation for other leaders in their global operations around the world. It felt amazing. About halfway through that multi-year project, I realized we hadn't yet overtly pulled in the company's mission statement, so I went looking for it. Essentially, the company's mission was simply to deliver shareholder value. That's it. All those people around the world were working hard, leaving families every day, and being asked to deliver above and beyond productivity, and at the end of the day, it was all in service of putting more returns in the pockets of wealthy shareholders. I was shocked because I'd been so encouraged by the positive culture our work was supporting, and I was naïve enough to believe there was more to the story than profit, than shareholder return. Needless to say, we did not weave that mission statement into our leadership development program. I just couldn't.

We need to release the idea that profit is the primary function of

---

56   "Women Now Hold 8.5% of Canada's Top Jobs," CBS News, March 19, 2015, https://www.cbc.ca/news/business/women-now-hold-8-5-of-canada-s-top-jobs-1.3001744.

business, and that shareholder value is a good enough reason for a business to operate, because that notion has excused all manner of social and environmental damage done by corporations. If we only evaluate the value of a corporation by how it performs financially and how much return it provides to shareholders, then we do not account for the true cost that business may have on communities and the environment. The shareholder-as-only-stakeholder model is outdated and frankly inaccurate. Businesses have impacts well beyond the financial—they impact our environment, communities and, in the case of large corporations, our societies. Innovative organizations today are instead thinking about both profit *and* purpose, shareholder return *and* employee needs *and* sustainability. Progressive companies are thinking about 360 degree stakeholders and circular economies, where all stakeholders, human and environmental, are considered, from resource consumption right through to disposal and management of waste. This kind of thinking is a mindset shift that we, as a society, have every right to demand and expect because we, too, are stakeholders in various ways. We've been told "this is just the way it is," but that is simply a choice that we've allowed, and we don't need to allow it anymore.

There are great tools emerging to qualify and quantify this multi-stakeholder approach to running organizations and corporations.

Conscious capitalism refers to a socially responsible economic and political philosophy. The premise behind conscious capitalism is that businesses should operate ethically while they pursue profits. This means they should consider serving all stakeholders involved, including their employees, humanity and the environment—not just their management teams and shareholders.[57] The Benefit Corporation (B Corp) movement uses their B Impact Assessment to provide concrete ways to identify and measure impact across factors like governance, workforce, supply chain, community and environment, and the results of this assessment then guide decision-making to ensure best decisions and impact for all stakeholders. [58] The Women's Leadership Intensive is a certified B Corp, and going through the Impact Assessment process helped me see where and how to build a company that was ethical, sustainable and equitable.[59]

New venture funding models like SheEO "[bring] together women and non-binary folks from all different backgrounds and ages, called Activators who contribute to a Perpetual Fund that is loaned out at zero percent interest to women + non-binary led Ventures who are working on the World's To-Do List, who are selected by the Activators."[60] The idea of supporting organizations with an intent to improve something in the world, align to the UN Sustainable Development Goals and work on the World's To-Do List is indeed radical, and it's gaining traction and attention from some of the big banks because it's been so effective, with far above average repayment rates and sustainable venture growth.[61]

---

57   Michelle Baker, "Benefit Corporations—A Move Away from Capitalism?" Neo Law Group, June 18, 2013, https://nonprofitlawblog.com/benefit-corporations-a-move-away-from-capitalism/.

58   "B Impact Assessment," B Lab, accessed May 27, 2022, **Error! Hyperlink reference not valid.**https://www.bcorporation.net/en-us/programs-and-tools/b-impact-assessment.

59   "The Women's Leadership Intensive," B Corp Movement, accessed May 3, 2022, https://www.bcorporation.net/en-us/find-a-b-corp/company/the-womens-leadership-intensive.

60   "About Us," SheEO, accessed May 3, 2022, https://sheeo.world/about-us/.

61   "What Is the World's To-Do List?" SheEO, accessed May 3, 2022, https://sheeo.world/what-is-the-worlds-to-do-list/.

The economy is not something academic or "over our heads." It's our daily experience of the world when we go to work, buy our groceries and try to send our kids to college. We're all a part of it, and the more we learn about it, the more we can impact it through how we participate in it, because participate we do, every day with every dollar we spend and save.

Some people do have a lot to lose if we change our economic models; the ones who are making it big, the millionaires and billionaires who influence most of the decisions about how the world of business and commerce runs. The very people who hold the power to change things are the ones who feel they have the most to lose by doing so. No wonder change has been slow.

So many other systems are based on and tied to our current economic models that it feels risky to rock the boat. Changing one system creates a ripple effect into all the other systems around it. This is why the world of work has remained structured much the same way for so long, even though our workforce has changed dramatically.

CHAPTER four

Work hasn't worked for a while now.

Men still run the world—and I'm not sure it's going that well.

— SHERYL SANDBERG[62]

Don't think about making women fit the world—think about making the world fit women.

— GLORIA STEINEM[63]

---

62   Stephanie Thomson, "Facebook COO: 'Men Still Run the World—and It's Not Going That Well,'" WeForum, January 20, 2016, https://www.weforum.org/agenda/2016/01/sheryl-sandberg-men-still-run-the-world-and-it-s-not-going-that-well/.

63   Cora Lewis, "Steinem Headlines Talk About Feminism," *Yale News*, February 1, 2010, https://yaledailynews.com/blog/2010/02/01/steinem-headlines-talk-about-feminism/.

I f we start to question the logic and inclusivity of our economic systems, it leads to a cascade of questions about all the other systems that support those economic systems, like the world of work. I was reading an article the other day that I've been thinking about ever since. It hypothesized that we humans are more able to imagine the apocalypse than we are to imagine a world not based on capitalism.[64] Interesting thought. Certainly, movies and books would reinforce that notion since there are a million books and movies about the end of days, dystopia and apocalypse, but I can't think of many that present an image of a very different but thriving world. Modern capitalism has evolved over four or five hundred years, but it's still just one way of looking at the world.

The 40-hour workweek was introduced in the 1800s as a way to limit the exploitation of workers, who were expected to work 80 to 100 hours per week at that time. In addition to being a workers' rights issue, there was some research even back then to suggest that working more than eight hours per day resulted in very little increase in productivity. There are diminishing returns as we push for more hours of work from our people. Sound familiar? Then, in 1938, U.S. Congress passed the Fair Labor Standards Act, which required employers to pay overtime to all employees who worked more than 44 hours a week. They amended the act two years later to reduce the workweek to 40 hours. In 1940, the 40-hour workweek became U.S. law.[65]

---

64 Nick Diaz, "Introducing Mark Fisher: Part 1—Capitalist Realism," Medium, August 29, 2021, https://medium.com/@nicholasadiaz7/introducing-mark-fisher-part-1-capitalist-realism-62e5a3861d53 .

65 Marguerite Ward and Shana Lebowitz, "More Leaders Are Scrapping the 40-Hour Workweek. Here's How It Became So Popular in the First Place," Business Insider, updated January 12, 2022, https://www.businessinsider.com/history-of-the-40-hour-workweek-2015-10.

We can argue whether eight hours per day, 40 hours per week is the optimal work expectation for either productivity or the health and well-being of employees. I am personally more productive when I work less than that. Some say 32 hours per week would be ideal. Regardless, there are other key factors about the way work is structured that are problematic for women in particular.

Thinking back to the 1800s and early 1900s, who do you think the structure of workplaces was built for? Like most things, work was built for men. And then, as now, most men in the workforce, and certainly those who made the rules, had support from the women in their lives. Wives, yes, but also mothers, sisters, assistants, housekeepers, etc. The expectation that someone could work 40+ hours per week and still do things like raise children, grocery shop, keep a house, maintain social and familial relationships and contribute to the community, all while having a hobby or having a life is simply not realistic. When men were the primary workforce, and when men had women to maintain the domestic and community obligations of a household, it seemed to work, particularly for the nuclear, heterosexual, middle-class family. Women without male partners or of lower socioeconomic status were a different story. But the narrative of the day was that the women did all that work behind the scenes, unpaid, unvalued and unrecognized, while the men went to work outside the home.

Although women are now working outside the home in almost the same numbers as men, unpaid and unvalued labour within the household continues to largely fall upon women. It's been called the "second shift" because all those household tasks didn't go away when there was no longer someone whose full-time job it was to manage them. We still need groceries and childcare and someone to remember Aunt Helen's birthday and take Grandpa to his doctor's appointment and on and on. And so many women have found ourselves working the equivalent of two full-time jobs, one outside the home and one keeping up with the responsibilities of our households.

Women entered the workforce and, by the 2020s, many households had two full-time working adults.[66] Women being in the workforce has been good for women and great for business. Women are some of the most capable, loyal, innovative, dedicated employees around. But most of the expectations around work have not changed on pace with the changing workforce. Women live very different lives and have very different demands on their time than men with wives used to have. When we take all the adults in a household and have them working outside the home for 40+ hours of the week, we have some major gaps. And that doesn't account for the reality that many of us work more than 40 hours, either because we need to economically, or because the expectations of work keep creeping and creeping further into our lives. There are all the unwritten rules and expectations that if you don't work all the time, if you're not available, then you're not committed, you're not promotable, you won't get ahead, and you may not even keep your job. Thank-you, capitalism and our current economic model (which values growth and greater productivity above all else).

So, the double-income household becomes common, and it works well for very few households. Who picks up the children when school is over at 3:00 p.m.? Who answers the call when a child or family member is sick and needs immediate help? Who remembers that it's

---

66   Alexia Fernández Campbell, "How Working Moms Are Changing American Households," *The Atlantic,* November 4, 2015, https://www.theatlantic.com/politics/archive/2015/11/how-working-moms-are-changing-american-households/433332/.

a holiday and they should plan a get-together, bake a cake and make sure everyone shows up? When do the groceries get picked up, and who figures out what to eat for breakfast, lunch and dinner (Every. Single. Day.)? Those with enough resources can hire out those services: before- and after-care programs for children, in-home support, grocery or meal-delivery services, etc. The more we work, the more we spend, and we just keep the merry-go-round endlessly spinning.

Ever feel like you can't quite make work work with your life? It's not you. It's because the workplace wasn't built by or for you. Work was built for a reality that most of us no longer live. It was built for households with an unpaid, in-house domestic labour force. It was powered by women supporting men. And rather than change the workplace to fit the changing workforce, we've persisted in expecting the workforce to fit the old, outdated standards and expectations of workplaces. Women have tied ourselves in knots in order to make it work. We've pumped breast milk in bathroom stalls and in our cars so we can feed our babies, we've raced from day-care drop-off to make it to meetings on time, we've gotten up at 5:00 a.m. to catch up on emails and stayed up until midnight cleaning the kitchen. We've been hailed as multi-tasking superwomen who can somehow be star performers at work while making mental grocery lists and looking after our aging parents. And it's killing us. We are exhausted. We are shattered.

Do you know what we're missing most? Joy. Peace. Time. Essentially, quality of life is what goes when the demands are constant and unrelenting. Women I talk to feel like they don't have time to do anything except get it all done, meet everyone's needs and expectations and then do it all over again the next day. The never-ending to-do list is a constant source of stress, and so many women feel like they're not being fully present or successful at work or at home.

Add in the global COVID-19 pandemic, and the whole system fell apart around our ears. When schools and day cares closed, when paid caregiving work became impossible to access due to shortages and lockdowns, the harsh realities of working while running a household became undeniable. Those of us who were able to work from home saw it unfolding on our Zoom screens, saw it in the faces of our colleagues who had to manage school at home while still meeting deadlines and attending meetings. Those who were front-line workers, so many of whom were women working in health care, retail and food services, still had to find a way to go to work when their children's schools and day cares were closed. The tenuous and illusory separation between work and home dissolved, and it was women who bore the brunt of that, women who now had to figure out how to meet the demands of work, which didn't diminish and didn't change, with the demands of children at home, full time. All the systems that those with resources had relied on went away. Those who didn't have the resources already knew what it was like, and the pandemic compounded it even further for them.

According to UN Women, Economic crises hit women harder. Here's why:

- ⊙ Women tend to earn less.
- ⊙ Women have fewer savings.
- ⊙ Women are disproportionately more in the informal economy.
- ⊙ Women have less access to social protections.
- ⊙ Women are more likely to be burdened with unpaid

care and domestic work, and therefore have to drop out
of the labour force.

⊙ Women make up the majority of single-parent
households.[67]

Women who are poor and marginalized face an even higher risk
of COVID-19 transmission and fatalities, loss of livelihood,
and increased violence. Globally, 70 per cent of health workers
and first responders are women, and yet, they are not at par
with their male counterparts. At 28 per cent, the gender pay
gap in the health sector is higher than the overall gender pay
gap (16 per cent).

…For domestic workers, 80 per cent of whom are women,
the situation has been dire: around the world, a staggering 72
per cent of domestic workers have lost their jobs. Even before
the pandemic, paid domestic work, like many other informal
economy jobs, lacked basic worker protections like paid leave,
notice period or severance pay.[68]

Women already knew that the myth of "having it all"—the expectation that women can work a full-time (or more) job while still
running our households like previous generations of women who
were not in the workforce in the same numbers—didn't do them
any favours. Greater work expectations came in, but the domestic
expectations didn't disappear or diminish. Everything compounded.
Women started burning out, and now so many of us feel like we

67   "COVID-19 and Its Economic Toll on Women: The Story Behind the Numbers," UN
      Women, September 16, 2020, https://www.unwomen.org/en/news/stories/2020/9/
      feature-covid-19-economic-impacts-on-women.
68   Ibid.

aren't doing justice to any domain of our lives. We were supposed to work like we didn't run households and run our households like we didn't have jobs. Impossible, but we just kept swimming.

Emily and Amelia Nagoski wrote a great book called *Burnout: The Secret to Unlocking the Stress Cycle*, and in it they describe that laboratory tests conducted on rats showed a difference in how male and female rats respond to stress. When intentionally stressed to elicit a stress response, the rats would then be put into a forced swim test to see how long they would be able to keep swimming. What researchers found was that the female rats kept swimming longer than the male rats, and they just kept on swimming. When stressed, they just kept trying, kept going. And I think that's what a lot of us human females are doing too.

> We have been taught that letting go of a goal is the same as failing. We share stories of people overcoming the odds to achieve remarkable things in the face of great resistance, which is inspiring. But these stories too often imply that we are the controllers of our destinies....

> Our tendency to cling to the broken thing we have rather than let it go and reach for something new isn't just a result of social learning. The stress (fear, anxiety, etc.) underlying the belief *changes our decision-making*, so that the more stressed we feel about change, the less likely we are to do it.[69]

Think about that for a second. The more stressed you are, the less likely you are to change. If women have been doing the "second

---

69   Emily Nagoski and Amelia Nagoski, *Burnout: The Secret to Solving the Stress Cycle* (New York: Ballantine Books, 2019).

shift" of coming home from jobs and caring for families, feeding people, signing permission forms for school, helping with homework, keeping the dog alive and keeping the floor clean and making sure the holidays are fun for everyone, and, and, and, then there's no doubt many women live in a state of near-constant stress. Then there's sexual harassment, seeing your male colleagues get promoted faster and make more money, the fact that you can no longer access an abortion for any reason if you live in certain states in the U.S., and the ever-present expectation that you should also be thin and beautiful. Damn right we're stressed. Thanks to the Nagoski sisters' research, if you've been blaming yourself for not being able to change your situation, you can let yourself off that hook. Your very stress level is preventing you from making the decision to change it. And it makes sense. When we're in survival mode, the idea of creating change is exhausting and scary. We simply persist on the path we're on and try harder. We keep swimming. To quote *Burnout: The Secret to Solving the Stress Cycle:*

> Massachusetts Senator Elizabeth Warren made news when…she was silenced by Senate Majority Leader Mitch McConnell… [She was attempting] to read a letter from Coretta Scott King about the racist judicial record of then-Senator Jeff Sessions. McConnell said, in what would become a notorious comment, "She was warned. She was given an explanation. Nevertheless, she persisted."
>
> …Whatever McConnell's motivation, women heard his words and recognized the ways they, too, had been silenced. "Nevertheless, she persisted" instantly became a rallying cry for women everywhere who had been told to sit down and shut up….

It resonated so powerfully because persisting is what women do, each and every day. Often we persist because we literally have no choice. We have children to feed and a world to change, and we can't just stop because it's hard....

But raise your hand if it gets exhausting. Raise your hand if you've wanted to quit. Raise your hand if you've asked yourself, *How much more do I have to do before I've done enough? How much of myself do I have to give? How smoothly do I have to polish myself before I can move through the world without friction?*

Us too.[70]

Now we're seeing the fallout in the Great Resignation and the anticipation of decades of labour shortages. At first glance, the Great Resignation seemed to be a result of the pandemic, but when researchers and writers started to dig into root causes it revealed a longer-term issue, toxic work culture and a lack of fulfillment from dedicating the majority of our working lives to workplaces or corporations that simply don't fit our values or humanity. The real issue here is we've always tried to force people, the workers, to fit the workplace, instead of changing the workplace to fit people. If we could decentre the "standard male worker" of the past around whom the workplace is still structured today, how might we build it differently? Fewer hours, flexibility, different ways of assessing performance that account for the diversity in roles and expectations for diverse workers? Even those relatively simple changes are not being made in many workplaces. Instead, we are given the distraction of committees and events, which are simply taking our focus away from the real system-

---

70   Ibid.

ic change that needs to happen.

> I have no patience for any kind of program or if a business or corporation talks about anything except their advancement in supplier diversity, wage equity, promotions and the pipeline, or diversity on their boards. That's all I want to hear about from you. Anything else, any other program, no, not interested. Because if you're putting money towards anything except those big issues, that's a waste of money and you're not doing anything. You're not doing the core work. So don't pat yourselves on the back because you have some committee that deals with sexual harassment. No. You know who deals with sexual harassment? The law. It's against the law. It's not an employee committee that talks about it. Equality between sexes and races, that's in the Charter of Freedoms. It's not aspirational. It's not something that we should hope for. It's law. So, we need to hold people accountable.

> Nancy Wilson, CanWCC interview, 2022[71]

An example of the kind of systemic change we're talking about is in ESG (environment, social / sustainability and governance) leadership. We're starting to see links between women's participation in leadership and sustainable thinking and decision-making.

> Women's participation in decision making is good for the planet: research shows a clear linkage between women's leadership and pro environmental outcomes. For example, countries with higher proportions of women in parliament are more likely to ratify international environmental treaties, to create protected

---

71   Interview with author, February 18, 2022.

areas, and to have stricter climate change policies. Countries where women enjoy greater social and political status have lower emissions and climate footprints.

Women's leadership style also favors long-term thinking, collaboration, transparency, and inclusion—in the Young Global Leaders (YGL) community this is manifested by the power of the "we." We need to recognize the contributions of women as decision makers, stakeholders, educators, and experts across borders and sectors to drive long-term solutions. It's time we realize women are the missing piece in our global efforts to protect and regenerate our planet.[72]

I was talking with a colleague the other day about co-developing a workshop on women leading sustainability. My colleague was lamenting the lack of willingness for change on the part of the leadership team at one of her client organizations. A young woman on her team dubbed it "willing confusion"—or maybe it was "willful confusion." Either way, you get the idea. The business case for change has been made in so many places—sustainability, inclusion, equity, you name it. But the change isn't happening. Why? Leaders are choosing to say that it's too complicated, that it will take time, to remain willingly confused so they can keep things the same instead of digging in and leading change. Make no mistake, the choice to not change, the choice to not act, *is* a leadership choice, a choice that is being made by many leaders today.

You may have heard that women today are less happy than previous

---

72   Mariah Levin, Gwendoline De Ganay, and Marga Soler, "Why Female Leadership Is Crucial to Tackling Climate Change and Other Crises," World Economic Forum, November 23, 2021, https://www.weforum.org/agenda/2021/11/why-female-leadership-is-crucial-to-tackle-climate-change/.

generations of their mothers and grandmothers, and it makes sense. Current generations of women are as squeezed as one can get between the demands of work and home. Thinking about our own happiness is often a distant dream, and "self-care" has been monetized into a multi-billion-dollar industry and has lost meaning for many of us. Some have used this as a rationale for why women should continue to be excluded from work; wouldn't they be happier if they had less pressure? Yeah, we would, but it's not about going back into the kitchen, it's about co-creating a work world that actually works for women too, one that works for the modern workforce, where most households do not have a stay-at-home adult.

The structure of work today is not all that different from early constructs of work. The idea of flexible work hours is still an uphill climb. As much as work from home was normalized in many industries during the pandemic, as the pandemic restrictions ease, many organizations are mandating employees back into the workplace, which means commutes and complications with childcare and other domestic responsibilities once more. As hard as it has been to have our workplaces in our dining rooms and bedrooms, at least we could throw in a load of laundry between meetings.

Most workplaces are structured as hierarchies because the military was an early model for how organizations should be structured. Workers are monitored, measured and controlled, just like early industrial engineering theories, which considered the workers to be cogs in the machine of the organization. Running the world like a military operation or an Industrial Revolution–era factory might have worked at one time, but it's a disaster today. The very nature of the work most people do today is so vastly different from that early thinking that it's a terrible fit in most cases.

I believe we have the creativity to come up with ways to change our current workplaces to make them fit the people, the diverse workforce we have today, and to build something completely different. There are examples of this we can learn and build from. Progressive business and working models experiment with things like self-management, horizontal organization structures, power sharing, shared decision-making, sustainability as a core decision filter, and going beyond "flexible hours" to self-determination in choosing how, when and where to work. These models are both risky and exciting, which is what makes them an adventure, an exploration of unknown territory.

Isn't it time we experimented with some new ways of working? We know what we're doing today isn't working anyway, so what have we got to lose? We often dismiss new models or ideas because they might be difficult or imperfect. Well, what we're doing today is also difficult and imperfect. We need leaders with the courage to try new things, knowing that the outcomes are not certain. We need leaders who are willing to experiment and trust that we'll figure it out because we humans are infinitely resourceful. We won't find new models that work unless we're willing to try and fail, learn what doesn't work, adapt and experiment some more. Many of us have ideas for how it could be different. If you're a leader or you have a scope of influence, perhaps it's time to start asking what your workforce wants to be different, develop some new ways, and try them out. Worst case, they don't work perfectly. That's okay, what we have now isn't perfect either. But even if the ideas don't work out the very conversation, the asking of the questions and listening to what people have to say, will make a difference.

CHAPTER five

Leaders shape culture, and who they are matters.

Women belong in all places where decisions are being made.
It shouldn't be that women are the exception.

— RUTH BADER GINSBURG[73]

L ook around your country, your community, your organization, your place of spiritual practice. Do the leaders there
look like you? Do they truly reflect the communities they
serve? If we were to take the leaders we see and extrapolate the cor-
responding populations they represent, we would assume that the

---

73   Bill Mears, "Justice Ginsburg Ready to Welcome Sotomayor," CNN Politics, June 16,
      2009, https://www.cnn.com/2009/POLITICS/06/16/sotomayor.ginsburg/index.html.

Western world is made up of a majority of some combination of white, middle-aged (or older) males—some combination of what has been called pale, male and stale—that's who's running this place at the highest levels. Google an image of "Premiers of Canada" or "US Senators" or "CEO's" and it will be painfully obvious what I mean.

And in theory, yes, any leader could lead well on behalf of different people, people who do not look like them or live like them, people from a variety of backgrounds and experiences, very different from their own. I've heard that argument many times, and I'm not arguing the converse. I'm not interested in the theoretical. I'm interested in what actually happens, and what generally happens is that our current leaders uphold systems and institutions that work well for them, which continues to perpetuate and reinforce those very same systems and institutions.

When I post content on social media about how we need more women leaders, how we need to vote for women, set goals and quotas to hire and promote women, what I get back is a lot of support but also a lot of backlash, some of it subtle, some not so much. The most common thing I hear is that we should be hiring the best person for each job, that it's not about gender. That's a nice argument when you belong to a group that holds the majority of leadership roles, highest-paid positions and political appointments. It's an argument that sounds egalitarian at first blush. It's kind of like how "all lives matter" is designed to sound like equality when in reality it ignores and dismisses white supremacy, anti-Black racism, inequity, shockingly disproportionate police violence and incarceration, and the maintaining of systems and institutions designed to keep some people in and some people out. The "best person for the job" argument completely ignores the inequality that exists. In our society, the "best person" has generally meant the "best man." The numbers don't lie.

Hans Rosling, a Swedish statistician that my son introduced me to through his fascinating TED Talks and videos, has a way of describing the situation that fit perfectly for me: he calls it "bad and better." Things are getting better, thankfully. But that doesn't mean we should relax or not worry or look away because many things are still bad. Things can be both bad and getting better at the same time. It's a both/and situation. It's both bad and better.[74] This way of looking at it brings me hope that we do have some solutions that are already starting to work; we are seeing improvements, things are getting better. Yay! But things are still bad, so let's keep working on making those bad things better.

Are things getting better for women in leadership? Absolutely. When I first started the Women's Leadership Intensive, most of my conversations were about why we even needed to develop women in leadership. The gap was unacknowledged and, in many cases, undiscussed. Today, almost everyone I speak to is aware of things like the gender pay gap and the leadership gap. The words *diversity*, *equity* and *inclusion* are part of most organizations' vocabularies and, in many cases, are getting attention and resources.

As an example of how things are getting better, there are more women CEOs of Fortune 500 companies pretty much every year, as this graph below from *Fortune* shows:

---

74   Hans Rosling, *Factfulness: Ten Reasons We're Wrong About the World—and Why Things Are Better Than You Think* (London: Sceptre, 2018).

Number of female CEOs in the Fortune 500 [75]

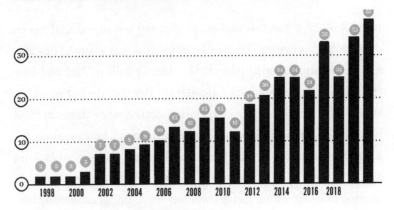

DATA FOR FORTUNE 500 LIST FROM 1998 TO 2020
EMMA HINCHCLIFFE, "THE NUMBER OF FEMALE CEOS IN THE FORTUNE 500 HITS AN ALL-TIME RECORD," FORTUNE, MAY 18, 2020, HYPERLINK "HTTPS://FORTUNE.COM/2020/05/18/WOMEN-CEOS-FORTUNE-500-2020/" HTTPS://FORTUNE.COM/2020/05/18/WOMEN-CEOS-FORTUNE-500-2020/.

I mean, just look at that curve. Things are looking good, right? It is indeed progress, and we should applaud and support every single one of those female CEOs and the companies that hired and promoted them. But as much as things are getting better for women in leadership, they're still pretty bad. This next graph adds the context in which those women CEOs live:

---

75   Emma Hinchcliffe, "The Number of Female CEOs in the Fortune 500 Hits an All-Time Record," *Fortune,* May 18, 2020, https://fortune.com/2020/05/18/women-ceos-fortune-500-2020/.

FORTUNE 500 CEOs *grouped by* GENDER

Women   Men

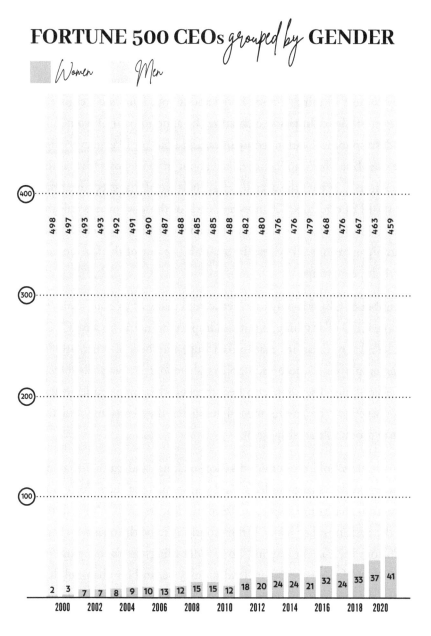

Year	Men	Women
2000	498	2
2001	497	3
2002	493	7
2003	493	7
2004	492	8
2005	491	9
2006	490	10
2007	487	13
2008	488	12
2009	485	15
2010	485	15
2011	488	12
2012	482	18
2013	480	20
2014	476	24
2015	476	24
2016	479	21
2017	468	32
2018	476	24
2019	467	33
2020	463	37
2021	459	41

SOURCE: FORTUNE
HTTPS://FORTUNE.COM/2021/06/02/FEMALE-CEOS-FORTUNE-500-2021-WOMEN-CEO-LIST-ROZ-BREWER-WALGREENS-KAREN-LYNCH-CVS-THASUNDA-BROWN-DUCKETT-TIAA/

The curve is moving in the right direction, *and* it's still nowhere close to being equal. If you were wondering how much work is left to do, this picture demonstrates it clearly. Celebrate the progress *and* keep this context in mind. I don't know about you, but I see a constant stream of LinkedIn posts celebrating the appointment of women in leadership roles at various companies, and I put my like on every single one. But what's not being talked about in those posts is what the backdrop is. What's the overall gender balance of that executive team or board of directors? Chances are, each of those women is still the vast minority in the leadership breakdown of their respective fields and organizations. They may be an "only" or one of the few women in their peer groups.

Number of CEOs is only one metric, and many of us don't aspire to be the CEO of anything, but it's an important metric because CEOs make a lot of decisions that impact huge numbers of other people: their employees, customers, suppliers, shareholders, and stakeholders of every kind. They impact others through the communities where they operate, the environmental resources they consume and the waste products they dispose of.

Our leaders hold economic, decision-making, and culture-shaping power. Leaders shape our lives. And yet, so many of them don't look like us or share our experience. Who our leaders are is a huge factor in the decisions they make. If they continue to be the ones who benefit from the current systems, no wonder things aren't changing. As liberal and feminist as Justin Trudeau may be, and I'm thankful that he is, the mistakes he continues to make and the scandals he's found himself involved in are due to blind spots that could be attributed to having been raised white, male and privileged in Canada. Sure, we can unlearn our blind spots and learn new perspectives, but why not simply include people who already have those different perspectives? Seems more streamlined. Why are we doing all this work to educate and expand the perspectives of privileged white men to enable them to keep their leadership positions, instead of just promoting and appointing a more varied group with a combined broader perspective? Unless of course there's a reason why being white, male and privileged equals leadership in our countries? We could say it was coincidence if the stats didn't paint such a definitive picture.

Which leaders speak for you, and which do not? The vast majority of decisions are still being made by the same handful of privileged leaders in business, politics, the economy and everywhere that matters. To become a leader takes resources. It might be money, education, status or connections. Or it might just be time, the most precious and rare resource for women across the board. The reality is that women and other excluded groups have less of all of these resources.

Remember, in Canadian politics, only 13 women have held the role of first minister (prime minister or premier) out of over 300. That's less that 5%, and women hold only 8.5% of the highest-paid positions in Canada. In the U.S., 2018 data shows:

5.3 percent.

Harvard Business Review says this proportion of large U.S. companies have CEOs named John—compared with 4.1 percent that have CEOs who are women.

Firms with CEOs named David, at 4.5 percent, also outnumber women-led businesses.

New numbers published in late April by *The New York Times*

showed many of the different leadership roles in the U.S., including politics, law, business, tech, academia, film and media, in which there are more men of a certain name represented than there are women, total.

For example, there are fewer women among Republican Senators or Democratic governors than there are men named John in those respective roles.

Additionally, the *Harvard Business Review* says 95 percent of CEOs are white men and 85 percent of board members and executives are white men.[76]

So, basically, if you're a white dude in America named John, you have a better chance at any of the leadership roles than *all* women combined. *All* of them. But sure, let's assume that's based on merit, not gender or race. In case you missed it, notice the combination maleness and whiteness here. John and David don't exactly top the list for racialized names.

Research in hiring has shown that as soon as we see a name on a resume and associate that name with the candidate being BIPOC or female, they will be more scrutinized and less likely to be hired. If we change the names or do blind interviewing, women and other excluded groups have a much higher chance of being considered on the actual merit of their resumes. We can let go of the notion that we're actually objective about these things. We're not, in any field or industry.

---

76   John Levesque, "For Large U.S. Companies, CEOs Named John Outnumber Total Number of Woman CEOs," Seattle Business, May 2018, https://seattlebusinessmag. com/workplace/large-us-companies-ceos-named-john-outnumber-total-number-woman-ceos.

For most of the twentieth century there were no female musicians in the New York Philharmonic Orchestra....But then all of a sudden, something changed: from the 1970s onwards, the number of female players started to go up. And up.

Turnover in orchestras is extremely low....So there was something remarkable going on when the proportion of women in the orchestra grew from a statistical 0% to 10% in a decade.

That something was blind auditions. Instituted in the early 1970s following a lawsuit, blind auditions are what they sound like; the hiring committee can't see who is playing in the audition, because there is a screen between them and the player.[77]

The *myth of meritocracy* is finally starting to be dismantled, although the arguments continue to come up whenever we get close to large-scale change, or worse yet, mandates for change in hiring or transparency of gender equity or lack thereof from corporations. Not only is the idea of meritocracy fatally flawed, but the very belief in it also perpetuates further discrimination:

Actually, a belief in meritocracy may be all you need—to introduce bias, that is. Studies have shown that a belief in your own personal objectivity, or a belief that you are not sexist, makes you less objective and more likely to behave in a sexist way. Men (women were not found to exhibit this bias) who believe that they are objective in hiring decisions are more likely to hire a male applicant than an identically described female applicant. And in organizations which are explicitly presented as meritocratic, managers favour male employees over equally qualified

---

77   Caroline Criado Perez, *Invisible Women*.

female employees.[78]

Men keep getting hired as our leaders because history, written and taught by men, has taught us to trust them more. To this day, many people actually believe that women are not as capable of running a company or a country—yes, they actually believe it and say it out loud when surveyed. Never mind all the unconscious biases out there! The overt bias is clear:

> The Reykjavík Index assesses attitudes toward female leadership in the G7 countries—Canada, France, Germany, Italy, Japan, the UK and the US—as well as India, Kenya and Nigeria. Its most recent survey of more than 20,000 adults led to some surprising and disheartening results.
>
> Only 38% of people in Japan were comfortable with the idea of a female head of government or a female CEO of a major company. In both Nigeria and Kenya, the scores (out of 100) were 62 for government and 56 for politics. The average G7 score for government and politics was higher, holding fairly steady over the last three years at 78. But this is still far from a score of 100—which would indicate that women and men are seen as equally suitable for leadership positions.
>
> Additionally, only 41% of people in Germany said they felt very comfortable with a woman being the head of government, in spite of Angela Merkel's long-time chancellorship. "It's just a myth that one female leader changes society," says Michelle Harrison, who leads the public division of Kantar, the market research company that runs the Reykjavík Index surveys. And

---

78   Ibid.

it's unrealistic to expect a single leader (woman or otherwise) to create sweeping change around gender roles.

Another striking finding was that around the world, young men were especially unlikely to endorse women leaders. This is surprising given that younger generations are often considered more progressive than older ones.[79]

Here's the thing. White men are not more capable of leadership. They are not more capable, period. They have screwed up, been imperfect, been mediocre, just like any other group of humans might be, and we've forgiven them and continued to hire, appoint and elect them. But we do not offer the same grace to women or racialized people. We have very different standards for them.

Black male leaders have said that they don't have the luxury of getting angry, making a mistake, or being imperfect, let alone surviving any of the scandals many of our white male leaders have been connected to while continuing to enjoy their leadership positions with all the associated power and pay. As soon as a Black man makes a misstep, the confirmation bias kicks in. "You see, I knew he wasn't qualified!"[80]

Same for women. You've heard of the glass ceiling. It's still very much in place, unshattered, as demonstrated by our abysmal numbers for women in leadership. Another phenomenon known as the "glass cliff" was proposed by Michelle Ryan and Alexander Haslam in

79   Christine Ro, "Why Do We Still Distrust Women Leaders?" BBC, January 19, 2021, https://www.bbc.com/worklife/article/20210108-why-do-we-still-distrust-women-leaders.

80   Lisa Roepe, "Barriers for Black Professionals," SHRM, February 6, 2021, https://www.shrm.org/hr-today/news/all-things-work/pages/racism-corporate-america.aspx.

2018. The glass cliff is the common practice of bringing on woman leaders when the chance of failure is high, when male leaders have screwed up long enough that the situation is a crisis, almost impossible to save. Then we demonstrate how liberal we are, how progressive, and we bring in the uber-qualified, perfectly groomed, usually white woman leader. The PR machines kick in. We celebrate the company, the industry, the jurisdiction that had the openness and generosity to finally give that woman a chance, and how confident we are that she can pull it out of the fire and save the day. Often, she is the first woman to hold the position, and often she is the only woman in her peer group. She is alone, on display and in a no-win situation.[81]

What happens? Well, the same thing that would happen to anyone in an impossible situation. More often than not, she fails. Or at least, she performs imperfectly. She cannot be above reproach in every decision; no one can. But the minute she steps one foot out of line, *boom*, she's done. The woman we hailed as the progressive choice to make us all feel better about equality ("See, it's not so bad, she's the first woman CEO of X or Y") is now in the "See, I told you so" category. These women do not get second chances.

Not only is it really hard for women to get to positions of leadership in any domain of our society, but it's also really hard to keep them because the standards are so impossibly high, and the obstacles and barriers so unacknowledged and unconsidered. Many women find that once they arrive at the position they worked so hard to get, they are up against another huge mountain of challenges and inequities,

---

81   Michelle Ryan and Alexander Haslam, "The Glass Cliff: Women Left to Take Charge at Times of Crisis," *The Times,* November 12, 2018, https://www.thetimes.co.uk/article/the-glass-cliff-women-taking-charge-but-at-times-of-crisis-czlvzzrns.

including public criticism, abuse, and threats of violence not experienced by their male counterparts.

One of the biggest losses with this continued lack of women in leadership roles at scale is we're missing out on the benefits that women leaders bring. We're going against the research yet again, because the research would show irrefutably that, when women participate in leadership, things get better for *everyone* on every metric—not just for women, but for *everyone*. Below are just a handful of examples you can find easily, and there are more the deeper you dig.

According to the Canadian Women's Foundation,

> A 2017 report suggests that steps to decrease gender inequality in the workplace may benefit Canada's economy by as much as $150 billion by 2026. If the gender gap was eliminated entirely, that number could rise to as high as $420 billion.

> High-performing businesses tend to have more women in leadership roles: 37% of leaders in higher-performing companies are women, compared to 19% of leaders in lower-ranked companies.

> Companies with the highest levels of diversity (either gender, ethnic, or racial) are anywhere from 15–35% more likely to have financial returns above their industry's national average.[82]

Women Deliver has found,

> When women are meaningfully represented and engaged

---

82   "Fact Sheet: Moving Women into Leadership," Canadian Women's Foundation, updated August 2017, https://fw3s926r0g42i6kes3bxg4i1-wpengine.netdna-ssl.com/wp-content/uploads/2017/09/Facts-About-Women-and-Leadership.pdf.

in leadership bodies—such as legislatures, courts, executive boards, and community councils—laws, rulings, and decisions are more likely to be inclusive, representative, and take diverse views into account.

Countries with a greater proportion of women as top decision-makers in legislatures have lower levels of income inequality.

Peace agreements are 35% more likely to last at least 15 years if women leaders are engaged in their creation and execution.[83]

And, finally, as Anna Daniszewski explains,

Research shows that when women are working in a company's management and leadership, there is a strong correlation with an improvement in their corporate social responsibility—such as better treatment of the environment, their employees, and those in their supply chain, and the creation of more ethical products, such as healthier foods.[84]

So why are we ignoring the data? Why do we continue to elect and promote almost exclusively men to positions of leadership in our society? We have a history to unpack, and deep biases and assumptions to uncover and unlearn. Even women. Even feminists. Because we were all raised in this patriarchal society, we all carry this learning inside us that we need to unlearn. We need to see it clearly and rec-

---

83 "Balancing the Power Equation: Women's Leadership in Politics, Businesses, and Communities," updated September 2018, https://womendeliver.org/wp-content/uploads/2018/09/Women-Leadership-Policy-Brief-9.23.18.pdf.

84 Anna Daniszewski, "5 Women Leading Change in Sustainable Business," accessed April 30, 2022, https://leadthechange.bard.edu/blog/5-women-leading-change-in-sustainable-business.

ognize it as just an idea we were taught, not truth.

But another important reason for this lack of large-scale change and the lack of inclusion of women in leadership is that those currently in positions of power make the rules and the decisions. And while theoretically those in power can make decisions to share that power and intentionally create equality, they often do not. They continue to hire, promote, sponsor and support others who look and think like them. If we hold on to the notion that this change will happen organically, change at scale is not going to happen, or it will take countless more generations to get there. Instead, we need strategic change. Legislation. Transparency. Quotas. Reporting. Or significant change will not happen in our lifetimes, nor in our children's.

Yes, I said quotas. Why not? Why is the idea of regulating equality so terrifying? What do we think we'll lose? Merit? Quality? There is absolutely no evidence to support that concern. In fact, just the opposite. The persistent belief that there isn't enough to go around makes it seem necessary to hold on tight to what we have, whether it's money, power, position, privilege. And the truth is yes, sharing is about redistributing power, position, wealth, so there could be loss for some who have the lion's share of that today. But the benefits that come from equality are benefits for *us all*. Gender equality has been shown to increase rates of education and access to health care; it's good for business and productivity; it's good for the environment, leads to better decision-making, greater peace and stability; all these things are good for all people. Sharing feels risky if you believe in scarcity, if you believe there's not enough so you need to protect what you have and not share it. Vicky Saunders describes the problem this way: "Well, it's the scarcity thing that's really bad, right? There's enough for everyone. It just isn't well distributed." What if scarcity simply wasn't true? What if we invited more people in instead of keeping them out?

As women, we know we have more to contribute. We know we have ideas about how things could be different and better. But we've been living with inequality all our lives, and we're tired. Part of the issue is that, as we move further into the world of work outside the home, the work inside the home and community has not gone away. Women still do the vast majority of domestic and caregiving work, and that means we are tired, under-resourced and very short on time. Not a great starting point to take on the world.

It's not just the structures of our workplaces that need to change, it's our households too. We need to stop looking at work and life as separate. What happens at home has a huge impact on how we participate at work, and what happens at work has a huge impact at home.

CHAPTER six

Equality begins at home.

*I am not free while any woman is unfree, even when
her shackles are very different from my own.*

— AUDRE LORDE[85]

*Women are not going to be equal outside
the home until men are equal in it.*

— GLORIA STEINEM[86]

85   "(1981) Audre Lorde, 'The Uses of Anger: Women Responding to Racism,'"
      BlackPast, August 12, 2012, https://www.blackpast.org/african-american-history/
      speeches-african-american-history/1981-audre-lorde-uses-anger-women-responding-
      racism/.
86   Steinem, *The Truth Will Set You Free, But First It Will Piss You Off!*, 32.

When I was a kid, I was very aware of the gender dynamics in my household. The roles and expectations were different for my mom and my dad, my brother and me. Sometimes those different expectations were quite subtle, other times not so much. As a result, I made two decisions in my child mind. First, I decided that if I had to choose whose life to model my own after, I would choose my dad's. I was never a fan of domestic or caregiving work. My mom worked in the family business, but she also did pretty much everything to do with the home and family. That didn't feel like me. But my dad ran the business and was out in the world; I wanted that. The second decision I made, and I didn't have a word for it at the time, was that I was a feminist. In my core, as a child, I believed that all genders should be equal, and I was starting to realize we weren't. I wonder if all children start out with a fundamental belief in equality until we socialize it out of them.

My earliest attempts at feminism were personal and angry. I didn't have language to describe the inequities I saw around me, and when I expressed them, I would inevitably be gaslit for being "emotional" in how I expressed my views, as though emotion and thought can't co-exist, as though a woman being angry immediately means her points are invalid. I felt powerless and like my perspectives were actively being dismissed and discounted. Like I was crazy. Like no one else saw what I saw or heard what I heard.

In high school, I cowrote a feminist rag for English class with the only one of my friends who seemed to notice that the world was gendered (and not in a good way). I pushed back against teachers who only used masculine language or examples. I recall clearly a math teacher who used only male sports examples. When I challenged him to use more inclusive examples, he made up a math problem about shopping "for the girls." I was furious. It was the '80s.

By the time I left high school, I had a full-blown identity crisis. What did it mean to be a woman in this world? All the things I was told I was supposed to be felt like acid in my gut. They made me itch. But if that wasn't what being a woman looked like for me, then what did it look like? I had no road map for being a young woman in a way that was authentic to me. All I saw around me were the blueprints we still see today for young women: be thin, be pretty, smile, be sexually available (but not too much, slut) and, most importantly, be likable. Don't challenge people (bitch), don't push back (man-hater), basically get in line and stay there—oh, and look good while you're doing it and *be nice*. Like most women, I grew up in a society that told me to accommodate, get along, be likable. How could I reconcile that need for approval with the fact that I saw the world as completely unfair?

> "The likability trap is still a thing." A recent *New York Times*/Siena College poll indicated that nearly 40% of respondents found all of the female candidates for president "just not likable" and many are drawing an inference from this that they may not be electable. Never mind the fact that President Trump is widely disliked, or that Hillary Clinton, who also struggled with likability, won the popular vote in 2016. Women continue to be dogged by the issue.

> …If likability for men means someone you want to have a beer with, for women it seems to be code for non-threatening, helpful and attractive.[87]

---

87   Hanna Hart, "Moving Beyond Likability: 5 Principles for Women Leaders That Men Can Learn From Too," *Forbes,* November 25, 2019, https://www.forbes.com/sites/hannahart/2019/11/25/moving-beyond-likability-5-principles-for-women-leaders-that-men-can-learn-from-too/?sh=34a54df67211.

In university, I hit rock bottom with an eating disorder and depression. I was trying to be inconspicuous and disappear in order to fit into a world I didn't fit into, and it was killing me. A friend introduced me to her aunt, Louise Walker, who would later become my lifelong best friend. And she introduced me to a women's group. It was the first time I had a truly supportive and truth-telling group of women in my life. It changed everything. The group wasn't perfect. It was what today would be described as white-centric and heteronormative, very "wife and mother" focused, which I was not. But it was the first time I experienced the power of women supporting other women, and it probably saved my life. When shit got hard, I had women to call. They picked up the phone, and we worked through it together. That's what women do.

In university, I was in a co-op science program. Most of the co-op jobs turned out to be incredibly boring and just reinforced that I was not cut out to work in a lab or in an office. Somewhere around third year, I applied for a job that I wasn't particularly qualified for but that was close to home and looked like actual fun: teaching outdoor science education at a summer camp program. That was a transformational moment for me. I had never realized there were jobs that were fun, healthy, outdoors. It was one of those defining moments when your path veers in a completely different direction. A left turn.

From that job, I went on to work in the school system in outdoor education programs, then eventually applied to work at Outward Bound. I had never gone camping or canoeing as a kid. I didn't know how to make a fire. I was on a steep learning curve, but I was smart and motivated by developing competence in those skills. To this day, I love technical competence and skill-building. It is truly empowering to get good at a technical skill.

I went from being terrified of heights to teaching climbing skills. It was my way of mastering the fear and not letting it control my options. I started working for a ropes course company, teaching technical and facilitation skills, and it was a fun and empowering job that I loved. During that time, I observed huge differences between the perceptions of male and female ropes course instructors. The company was co-owned by a man and a woman, and I co-instructed with both. When I co-instructed with the woman, the participants had no choice but to look to women for both technical and facilitation skills-building, advice, and information. But when I worked with the man, participants almost exclusively turned to him for anything technical or "hard skills" related, and to me for anything facilitation or "soft skills" related. I had observed the same thing working at Outward Bound when I worked in co-ed instructor pairings.

I was working on my Master of Education in Workplace Learning and Change, so I created a short survey for a course I was taking at the time and conducted some small-scale research on the differences in perception between male-female and female-female ropes course instructor pairings. That work was subsequently published in the *Journal of Experiential Education* in spring 2002.[88] It was an empowering experience to be able to put quantitative and qualitative data behind something I'd been experiencing all my life but hadn't previously had language to describe.

By 2000, I was done with co-ed instructor situations in outdoor education. I couldn't stomach another experience of not being heard

---

88   Belinda Clemmensen, "An Exploration of Difference and Perceptions of Difference Between Male and Female Challenge Course Instructors," *Journal of Experiential Education* 25, no. 1 (2002): 214–219, https://doi.org/10.1177/105382590202500105.

about any of the hard-won technical expertise I had developed over years in the field. I was sick of being more qualified than my male co-instructor but being ignored or dismissed or having my contributions downplayed or simply not seen. One of the things I loved about outdoor expedition was weather and navigation. I remember sitting on a rocky island in Georgian Bay, leading a co-ed adult sea kayak trip, when one of the male participants asked about why the wind always seemed to get stronger on the bay in the late afternoons. I explained about the difference in how land and water heat up during the day and retain heat, and how that differential means that the hot air rises, creating a void into which cool air floods, and voila, you have local wind patterns. Once I had spoken, the man turned to my male co-instructor and asked the question again, as if I hadn't spoken. And my male co-instructor answered, as if I hadn't spoken. I was done. It was just one example of so many.

I left Outward Bound in search of a way of being in the outdoors that was less masculine. I had taken a feminism course as part of my master's degree and wanted to apply feminist principles to my work in the outdoors. With four other highly skilled women who worked in outdoor leadership, and eventually a whole community of other skilled women, we started a fundraising and sea kayaking expedition project called Paddle to a Cure: Journeys of Hope. Our plan was to lead trips for the summer of 2000 to fundraise for breast cancer research and education and bring breast cancer survivors and their supporters on one of several sea kayak trips. The trips would be supported by sponsors for gear, food, etc., and they would be an opportunity to go to the wilderness to heal, regroup, grieve, form community and be in the beauty of the Canadian wilderness. Our commitment was to the quality of the experience above all else, and our principles included accessibility, inclusion, community contribution and engagement, shared decision-making, best practices in safety and sustainability, and raising money to support women's health. We planned for one epic summer, but we ended up running for five years and raising almost a million dollars. One of the most important outcomes from that experience was that I learned that a feminist organization model can work and create amazing outcomes.

All of this leads me to the topic of equality at home. I met the man who would become my partner around the time I was doing Paddle to a Cure. He and I worked together on some trailer repairs that first summer, and it felt like a partnership. I felt like he respected my skills and leadership and wasn't trying to "teach me" stuff. Mansplaining wasn't a term back then, but it was definitely a thing. Shane didn't mansplain stuff to me, and that in itself was a unique experience. He knew that in this situation, Paddle to a Cure, I was leading, and he was supporting, and he was good with it. He didn't need to assert himself or prove anything. Although I wasn't looking for a partner at the time, that dynamic was refreshing, and it stuck with me.

Over time, we got closer. In the back of my mind, I had decided long ago that I would not be getting married and setting up some kind of heteronormative household. I just couldn't see how I could reconcile that with who I was. I was not going to become somebody's wife, as I understood the role from everything I'd seen. I was not going to become domesticated. No thank you. I was a free woman, an adventurer, a feminist. And I couldn't see how I could continue to be those things in a marriage. I had no examples from which to see how that might be possible. Turns out, it is. But only with the right partner.

We got hitched. He proposed to me one New Year's Eve as we were drunkenly walking home from somewhere. I wasn't sure he was serious, but it got me thinking. I thought about it for a while. I don't remember exactly how long, but it was probably weeks. I thought, *Can I do this?* As much as I loved Shane and had no interest in leaving him, the idea of marriage scared me.

We raise women to believe their lives aren't complete without a partner. Their worth isn't secured until someone wants them. We joke about how men are afraid of commitment and women want a man, but not the other way around. In fact, men thrive in marriages. They are healthier, have higher earnings, more assets, more job stability and even live longer.[89] And why wouldn't they? In most heterosexual partnerships, women take good care of men. Women do most of the household labour, caregiving work and household management. Women take more parental leaves and downshift careers in order to raise the shared children. And with the majority of women also working outside the home, all of that happens without the former pressure on men to be the main "breadwinners" of the household.

> Women in the United States spend two hours more each day cleaning, cooking, taking care of children and doing other unpaid work than men, according to a report by Oxfam and the Institute for Women's Policy Research.
>
> The study, which analyzes data from the Bureau of Labor Statistics' American Time Use Survey, found that women aged 15 and older spend 5.7 hours daily doing housework and looking after kids and elders, while men in the same age range do so for 3.6 hours each day. That's about 37% more time dedicated to

---

89   "Why Are Men Overlooking the Benefits of Marriage?" ScienceDaily, February 7, 2017, https://www.sciencedaily.com/releases/2017/02/170207135943.htm.

keeping things running smoothly in the house.[90]

Those are just the extra hours of hands-on work. What about the constant mental load of figuring out healthy meals, remembering birthdays and other milestones, managing social calendars, etc.? In her book *Fair Play*, Eve Rodsky looks at heterosexual families with children and breaks it down like this:

> Mental Load: The never-ending mental to-do list you keep for all your family tasks. Though not as heavy as a bag of rocks, the constant details banding around in your mind nevertheless weigh you down. Mental "overload" creates stress, fatigue, and often forgetfulness. *Where did I put the damn car keys?*
>
> Second Shift: This is the domestic work you do long before you go to work and often even longer after you get home from the office. It's an unpaid shift that starts early and goes late, and you can't afford to lose it. *Every day's a double shift when you have two kids' lunches to prep!*
>
> Emotional Labour: This term has evolved organically in pop culture to include the "maintaining relationships" and "managing emotions" work like calling your in-laws, sending thank-you notes, buying teacher gifts, and soothing meltdowns in Target. This work of caring can be some of the most exhausting labor (akin to the day your child was born), but providing middle-of-the-night comfort is what makes you a wonderful and dependable parent. *It's OK, Mama's here.*

---

90 Drew Weisholtz, "Women Do 2 More Hours of Housework Daily Than Men, Study Says," TODAY, January 22, 2020, https://www.today.com/news/women-do-2-more-hours-housework-daily-men-study-says-t172272.

Invisible Work: This is the behind-the-scenes stuff that keeps a home and family running smoothly, although it's hardly noticed and is rarely valued. *The toothpaste never runs out. You're welcome.*[91]

I hear this played out time and again from the women I work with in my leadership programs. These are accomplished, successful women, and they tell stories of never having a spare moment between work and home demands, all while feeling guilty for not also being able to keep all the balls in the air with a smile on their faces and remaining thin, pretty, likable, sexually available and on and on and on. These women are exhausted, and it's robbing them of their joy. Working women, working moms, rarely have spare time, hobbies, bandwidth, or time to think. They are keeping the wheels on the bus 24-7.

So how did all this pan out for me, a feminist in relationship with a feminist partner? I won't lie, it hasn't always been easy. In the early days of our relationship, we worked some shit out. On kayak trips, Shane initially tried to impress me with his skills. It only pissed me off because I felt like he was ignoring the years of mastery I had built. But, after a few arguments on islands in the middle of the Great Lakes, we figured it out. He could impress me not by being the traditional male "expert," but by being side by side with me and being a feminist too. He wasn't raised that way, but he inherently believed in the logic of equality, learned more about it and is now one of the most supportive feminist male allies I know. He's always learning, as are all of us who are trying to unpack, unlearn and reprogram our deep socialization.

---

91   Eve Rodsky, *Fair Play: A Game-Changing Solution for When You Have Too Much to Do (and More Life to Live)* (New York: G.P. Putnam's Sons, 2019).

Then we had a baby. Gabe. Our hearts, our love. And boom, I was dropped from the self-chosen feminist world I had created into the oldest, most deeply socialized feminine role there is: mother. It was a supremely uncomfortable fit for me. Everyone had an opinion on my body, my pregnancy, my mothering approach, my decisions. Advice flowed freely, unbidden, from all corners. I couldn't get my feet under me for months after a difficult labour, emergency C-section and subsequent blood loss due to hemorrhaging. Worse yet, Gabe was born with a tiny hole in the lining around his heart and was taken immediately to the neonatal intensive care unit at a different hospital. There was no bed for me there, and I couldn't be discharged due to the trauma of the delivery. I was alone and was physically and emotionally wrecked.

But here is where the journey of Shane as a father begins. Shane went with Gabe to the other hospital. He started Gabe's life as the primary parent, the holder, feeder and rocker of the baby. As hard as that was on me, it was beautiful for them. They bonded in a way usually reserved for mothers. Within a couple of days—the longest of my life—my boys both came back to me, and we were together. Thankfully, Gabe took to nursing and I was able to breastfeed, which felt really important for me.

Whenever Shane and I had talked about having kids, I was super clear that it would have to be a fully joint effort. I was not the person who wanted to stay home all the time, who was interested in domestic life. I wasn't even particularly interested in the "year off" of parental leave that we have access to in Canada, although I was thankful for it and fully support it. I can't imagine starting a baby's life with only a few weeks or months of having a parent at home. And I definitely question if people who refer to parental leave as "time off" have ever spent long days and nights with a newborn.

I have always been proud of how Shane and I co-parented, right from the beginning. We both changed diapers, we both dealt with the crying and rocking and sleeplessness. Shane would get up in the night. When Gabe was old enough to call for someone in the night, it was Daddy. Why is that such a strange and almost shameful thing for a mother to admit? Because we've been socialized to think of parenting as "women's work."

Shane experienced adoration and praise for his active fathering, and incredulity at all he was doing as a co-parent. People were shocked that he would get up in the night to answer the cry, change a diaper and bring the baby to me for nursing. Shocked that he would be disturbed from his slumber, when, after all, he was the one "working." He was praised as an amazing dad because he changed his share of diapers or, God forbid, spent time alone with his own child! Seriously, this isn't even that long ago; Gabe was born in 2005.

We've heard more about this phenomenon in recent years, the idea that dads get accolades for doing the parenting work that women have been expected to do forever. Not only are women expected to do it without recognition, but we are constantly criticized for not doing it right, not doing enough, not being enough.

I promise you this. Nobody ever told me how great a mother I was when I changed a diaper, or made dinner, or got through the day on my own with a newborn. Nobody praised me for surviving years of interrupted sleep. Nope. That shit was just expected. It was Shane who was the hero parent every time he got out of his chair. And it pissed me off to no end. Shane didn't see it at first, but we talked about it and then he couldn't un-see it. He started correcting people who praised him. He would let them know he was simply parenting, same as me, and ask why they thought it was so much more heroic than anything I did. He had my back, but the world all around us did not.

On the flip side of that praise for being such a great dad, Shane also became tuned in to how excluded dads can be from the parenting landscape. People would turn to me, not Shane, with questions or conversations about kids. Parent support groups or baby-parent activities all seemed to be for moms. People were constantly surprised when it was Shane who showed up, baked the cupcakes for the school event or knew more about Gabe's schedule than I did. The world was not set up for equal parenting.

And that doesn't even begin to cover the inequities in other parts of the world.

> From cooking and cleaning, to fetching water and firewood or taking care of children and the elderly, women carry out at least two and a half times more unpaid household and care work than men. As a result, they have less time to engage in paid labour, or work longer hours, combining paid and unpaid labour. Women's unpaid work subsidizes the cost of care that sustains families, supports economies and often fills in for the lack of social services. Yet, it is rarely recognized as "work." Unpaid care and domestic work is valued to be 10 and 39 per cent of the Gross Domestic Product and can contribute more to the economy than the manufacturing, commerce or transportation sectors.[92]

---

92   "Women's Economic Empowerment in the Changing World of Work: Report of the Secretary-General," United Nations Digital Library, December 30, 2016, https://digitallibrary.un.org/record/856760?ln=en.

What all this boils down to is the fact that, as women have entered the workforce in greater numbers—"In 2019, Canadian women 15 years and older represented nearly half (47.4%) of the labor force, compared to 37.6% in 1976—a percentage increase of over 25%."[93]— our domestic and caregiving responsibilities have not decreased at pace. We are doing the jobs outside the home in the same numbers as men, but our home lives are not the same. Women do the majority of domestic, unpaid work, including the majority of caregiving, whether for children, elders, or others in our communities. We are doing the second and third shifts of unpaid, unrecognized work— and we are tired!

How do we then take on the work of change? Where will we find the energy and the time to take on leadership roles, fight for equality, change culture and policy, create a more equitable world for our children, when we are so tired and so overwhelmed by the constant practical and mental to-do lists in our lives?

Unfortunately, the answer is the same as it always is. We will fight for change because we must. Because it matters. We do it because it needs doing, and we have built that hard-won skill set, the ability to get shit done because it needs doing.

No matter what work we do out in the world, we won't have the equality we seek until we also shift the balance in our homes. A lot of the behaviour patterns of men and women in the home come from early socialization, so they run deep. It's expectations from our own parents, watching those early TV shows where the mom puts dinner on the table every night, seeing how our families of origin operate

---

93   "Women in the Workforce: Canada (Quick Take)," Catalyst, August 19, 2020, https://www.catalyst.org/research/women-in-the-workforce-canada/.

and then unconsciously repeating those patterns. The first step is to notice, to become conscious of the patterns. Maybe you live in a very fair and balanced household. Great. Maybe not. Okay. But we need to bring awareness to it, and that can be painful at first.

Here's a story that may sound familiar. Say my partner and son didn't notice that something needed to be done—for example, the floors needed vacuuming. In the past, I would get out the vacuum myself and then be angry and resentful about it. I called it "angry cleaning," and it didn't feel good. But I recognized it as a behaviour pattern that I'd learned. I'd seen other women do the same thing. That realization also didn't feel good, but it led me to my next step: ask. If the floors need vacuuming, I just ask my partner or son to vacuum the floor. It's not perfect because I'm still the one who noticed and asked, but it's shifting from "I'll just do it myself" and be angry about it to re-balancing the labour at home.

So, step one is notice, step two is ask. Part of asking is stopping ourselves from automatically jumping in to do things ourselves. We do that for a few reasons. One is out of necessity we have learned to be really efficient at these things and we get shit done. But another is that we too have been conditioned to believe it's on us to do these things. So, along with the practical steps of noticing and asking, there is also some unlearning and rewiring that needs to happen.

In my household, we have conversations about division of labour and try to change the systems that we've unconsciously been repeating. Last holiday season, I recognized (noticing) that as equal as our household was in many ways, holidays were not one of them. I still did the majority of planning the gatherings, the meals, the gifts, the wrapping, etc. We sat down and made a master list of all the things that go into making a nice holiday season for everyone, then we divided that list in three. Each of us got to check off the items we would do, and it was equal. I tell you, it was the most relaxed holiday I've had in my entire life as an adult woman. Why didn't we do that sooner? Partly because I'd never seen it done. I'd only seen my mother, aunts, grandmothers and women friends taking on all the work of holidays.

I get that I have a household where we're already talking about equality and it's basically what I think about all day as part of my job. There is receptivity to the idea of fairness at home that some of you may not have. That's why I say to start with noticing and asking. That might take some things off your plate and free up a bit more time and space for you, while also beginning to recondition the others in your household about the distribution of household labour and expectations of who does what. When we ask, we make the invisible visible. Okay, you didn't see the job of vacuuming before, you didn't see that it needed to be done or that you should be the one to pick up the vacuum and do it. Now I've asked you so it's visible. You now know it needs to be done and that it will be you to do it. If I ask you enough times, and you vacuum enough times, it becomes a new expectation, a new normal.

The worst thing we can do is silently keep everything running in the background, because that keeps it invisible, and what isn't seen isn't valued. Make the list, divide up the chores, have the conversations about why everyone should do their fair share, ignore the inevitable teenage (and other!) complaints, and get on with it. That in itself is work, but it's an investment in re-ordering the expectations around household labour which should free you up in the long run, both in terms of your time and your mental and emotional bandwidth.

Hopefully, you can also start having the kinds of conversations that unpack why we've had the expectations we've had and how to change them, especially if you have kids to educate. The work of equality in the home is not only in service of the women and other adults in the household, but also in service of our children. If we allow our households to perpetuate the notion that women do all that work, unpaid and largely invisible, then we are teaching our sons and daughters to do the same. We are teaching our sons to expect a woman to do that work, and we are teaching our daughters that to be good women they must handle all the domestic labour on behalf of everyone. I don't know about you, but I can't live with that.

CHAPTER seven

How do we change the world? One person at a time.

One of the criticisms I've faced over the years is that I'm not aggressive enough or assertive enough, or maybe somehow, because I'm empathetic, it means I'm weak. I totally rebel against that. I refuse to believe that you cannot be both compassionate and strong.

— JACINDA ARDERN[94]

Never doubt that a small group of thoughtful, committed citizens can change the world. Indeed, it is the only thing that ever has.

— MARGARET MEAD[95]

94   Maureen Dowd, "Lady of the Rings: Jacinda Rules," *The New York Times,* September 8, 2018, https://www.nytimes.com/2018/09/08/opinion/sunday/jacinda-ardern-new-zealand-prime-minister.html.
95   Mary Bowman-Kruhm, *Margaret Mead: A Biography* (Connecticut: Greenwood Publishing Group, 2003): 141.

Women are tired from pulling the double and triple shifts, from living in the unprecedented times of a global pandemic, and from ongoing conflict and war. Maybe we're feeling beyond shattered about the state of the world. Damn, I get that. But I keep coming back to that major wake-up call of looking at the world around me and thinking, *Well, this place needs some work.*

I was so busy as a younger working mom that I didn't really have the time or energy to truly lift my head up for some time. But as my son becomes older, that balance changes, and I start to think more about the world he is growing up into. I sometimes hear people in my own age group and older say things like, "The youth will inherit this world so it's up to them to change it." And I think, *Oh hell no! Leaving the mess we and former generations created for our children to deal with? That's the most irresponsible thing I've ever heard.* We're the group of people who currently hold the most power and money and resources and influence and access and everything, but we're just going to abdicate all responsibility to the young people?

Don't get me wrong, I actually believe we need more young people running this place. Absolutely we do. They need to be empowered, funded, supported and resourced to do so. Right now, that's not the case. There's the argument that, somehow, they don't understand the "real world," so they're not equipped to make good decisions. I call bullshit on that. Exactly whose "real world" are we talking about? Because those who shape the world get to tell the story of what the "real world" is like, and, frankly, I don't agree. Every time we have an election they hold a mock election at my son's school, and every time the young people vote in the Green party. And yet, they live in a Province where the Green party got one out of 124 seats in the legislature in 2022. I would love to see what would happen if those young people were running this place! The conversations on climate crisis alone would be completely different.

All of this converged into a bit of a mantra for me. It went like this: *I will be damned if I don't at least try to leave this place better than I found it.* If I've worked all these years and been fortunate enough to gain some resources, to gain a voice, gain the safety and privilege to use that voice, to live a life relatively free of oppression and violence, how could I squander that by doing nothing with it? Buying more stuff? A bigger house? Excuse me, but no way. That is a waste of resources. Addressing some of these crisis-level issues today—instead of leaving them for future generations—will take people who have resources choosing to use them for change rather than holding on to them for our own continued security or gains. Keeping all our resources for ourselves is being part of the problem, not part of the solution. We could make the road to change and equity so much smoother for those who come with us and after us by using our relative security, resources and voices to push hard for systemic change today.

Maybe this is a wake-up call for you too. Maybe you've bought into the story that your job is done, and now you can relax and spend your days being a good consumer and doing what you like because you've worked hard all your life, which you probably have. But the bad news is you're not done. Absolutely not. This is a perfect time to become an activist, by which I simply mean taking action for the improvements you wish to see in the world. It is absolutely on us to do this work. To clear a path for the others to step into. To make the road less steep for those coming with and coming next.

The feeling of overwhelm and powerlessness that we feel in the face of these big systemic problems is very real. We ask ourselves, "How can I possibly make a difference against this huge machine? These systems? These institutions?" And yet, one person at a time getting into action is really the groundswell for all social change.

The bottom line is that it's not up to someone else, and if we wait for someone else to do it, it won't get done. It's up to each one of us. And yes, it's hard, and we're exactly the people who may have been discouraged and disempowered and told not to make waves. And yet, it will take each one of us to connect to what we value and what we want for the world and then activate accordingly.

The starting point is to trust what you know. If you look at the world and you know something is not right, you feel it in your bones. We feel that something is not right, and we are disturbed. That's your clue. It is the place to investigate because it's pointing at something you care about, and that is where the motivation to use our voice, our resources, our passion for change comes from. It starts inside as a knowing, becomes a trusting of what we know, and then blooms into action, sometimes feeling like it becomes actions we can't *not* take, or things we can't leave unsaid.

Tarana Burke started the Me Too Movement in 2006. It wasn't until 2017, when it got picked up by women in Hollywood with exceptional influencer status, that it blew up and became the hashtag that we all know today. In the prologue of her book, *Unbound: My Story of Liberation and the Birth of the Me Too Movement*, she writes:

> Back in 2005 when I started working on "me too," it was so difficult to get people on board—including those who claimed to be in the service of our community. Activists, organizers, youth workers, social justice warriors, and the like would agree that it was necessary work, and congratulated me for taking it on,

but they still wouldn't do much to support or further our efforts. What motivated me to continue were the little Black and Brown girls who trusted us with their secrets, their pain, their shame, their worries, their anger, their fears, and their hopes.[96]

And that's it right there. Tarana Burke made the decision to do the work, to take her talent, resources, voice, leadership, skills and abilities and try to make something better. She saw the need clearly. She knew it and she chose not to look away or walk away. She didn't do it expecting that it would become what it did. Rather, she did it because she looked at the world and saw a place where it needed fixing, and she chose to set aside all the doubts that I'm sure she had, just like we all do, and get to work on it—imperfectly, with commitment, and knowing that she would not get fully supported by those around her, that there might be some very lonely times. She believed in her ability to make a difference, even if that difference was on a small scale, person by person, girl by girl. It didn't stay small, we know that now, but we have to be willing to go in and trust ourselves, and trust that the choice to make a difference, regardless of scale, is a worthy pursuit. And we are worthy of choosing it. In fact, we are built for it. Tarana also says in the prologue (believe me, the rest of the book is great too, but right from the prologue she gets down to it!):

The courage that trickled out of a young Black girl in the Bronx, and now from millions of others, formed the massive ocean that this movement has become. The essence of "me too" is found deep in the marrow of this lifelong story. There is no *here* without where I was: stuck and scared and ashamed,

---

96   Tarana Burke, *Unbound: My Story of Liberation and the Birth of the Me Too Movement* (New York: Flatiron Books, 2021).

a place I remained until the need to care for someone else's shame saved me too.[97]

Many of us are so busy surviving and managing all the demands of our day-to-day lives that we don't even know what we value or want to change. We get too busy to go inside and reflect, ask the deeper questions and understand the core of what we value and want for ourselves, our children and the world. It's one of the main things we work on at the Women's Leadership Intensive, asking ourselves the hard questions, the deep questions, the ones we're not even sure we want to know the answers to because then what?

We all need times of reflection and realization like I had as I was coming up on 50. We need to reflect on what matters most to us in this world and move into a place of action, because there is no "they will do it." There is only we. We all have a purpose that we want to fulfill. The word purpose can be intimidating, but I think of purpose as simply that place where meaning meets action. Where what matters to us turns into a commitment, and we start aligning our actions to our deeper values.

Where is that place for you? That's what we'll explore in the next chapter.

---

97   Ibid.

CHAPTER eight

Purpose: You're here for a reason. Lead with that.

You are allowed to take up space. Own who you are and what you want for yourself. Stop downplaying the things you care about, the hopes you have. Own your passions, your thoughts, your perceptions. Own your fire. Stop putting your worth in the hands of others; stop letting them decide your value. Own saying no, saying yes. Own your mood, your feelings. Own your plans, your path, your success.

— BIANCA SPARACINO[98]

We need to reshape our own perception of how we view ourselves. We have to step up as women and take the lead.

— BEYONCÉ[99]

---

98   Bianca Sparacino. *The Strength in Our Scars*. Brooklyn, NY: Thought Catalog Books, 2019.
99   *Life Is but a Dream*, directed by Ed Burke and Beyoncé Knowles (2013: United States: HBO).

Women have lifetimes of training and socialization to go along and get along. It's what we've been overtly valued for, and it's how we've stayed safe. And threats to our safety are still a huge concern for so many women. Early research into stress or threat responses (apparently only men were studied—we are no longer surprised) gave us the idea of fight-or-flight. Then we realized that running or getting aggressive weren't the only human responses to threats. Some people shut down not only physically, but mentally as well. We literally can't process; our minds go blank. This led to an update of our understanding of the stress response: fight, flight or freeze. But there are other ways we respond to threats and, based on our social status, many women instead respond with something called "tend-and-befriend," or something called "fawn."

> The human stress response has been characterized, both physiologically and behaviorally, as "fight-or flight." Although fight-or-flight may characterize the primary physiological responses to stress for both males and females, we propose that, behaviorally, females' responses are more marked by a pattern of "tend-and-befriend." Tending involves nurturant activities designed to protect the self and offspring that promote safety and reduce distress; befriending is the creation and maintenance of social networks that may aid in this process. The biobehavioral mechanism that underlies the tend-and-befriend pattern appears to draw on the attachment-caregiving system, and neuroendocrine evidence from animal and human studies suggests that oxytocin, in conjunction with female reproductive hormones and endogenous opioid peptide mechanisms, may be at its core. This previously unexplored

stress regulatory system has manifold implications for the study of stress.[100]

Many women tend and befriend in times of threat or stress. "Fawn" is another threat response, sometimes associated with trauma, although I can see how women manage everyday threats with fawning too. The writer Kyra Evans describes it this way: "Some people respond to feeling unsafe by withdrawing or lashing out. Others, like me, sense that we are not safe with someone and immediately feel the urge to pacify, coddle, and compliment the very person who has made us feel unsafe. This is called a fawn response."[101] All this to say, if we have learned to survive and stay safe by tending, befriending and sometimes fawning, those are natural, human, often female, responses to a sometimes-threatening world. The problem is those responses can sometimes be at odds with the need to challenge or create change. There have been so many times I froze, shut down or kept the peace when someone behaved badly or said something unacceptable, and then later I thought of all the sharp, intelligent and powerful things I should have said. But in the moment, I was keeping safe. It was only later, when I got back into a safe space, that my brain could think of all the alternative responses that would have been stronger, more effective, more empowering. Many women tell me they do the same thing.

We're still telling little girls that being pretty is their job, that girls are good when they are nice. And this dogs us through adulthood. We may be accomplished in our careers, look after children and elders,

---

100   Shelley Taylor et al. "Behavioral Responses to Stress in Females: Tend-and-Befriend, Not Fight-or-Flight," *Psychological Review* 107, no. 3 (2000): 411–429, https://doi.org/10.1037/0033-295X.107.3.411.

101   Kyra Evans (@kyra_evans_writer), "When we talk about survival responses (fight, flight, freeze, fawn), we're always talking about feeling safe and unsafe. For many of…" Instagram, February 10, 2022, https://www.instagram.com/p/CZzNIbHOHAC/.

run a household or a corporation or a marathon, but we know deep in our bones that regardless of any of this, the world still expects us to also be pleasant. In line.

That broad expectation, and our collective internalization of it, has been really helpful in maintaining the systems and power structures of our world. It's created the conditions in which we've accepted all kinds of ridiculousness from our leaders and those in power. It's created the conditions where we as women are complicit in gender stereotyping, discrimination and the policing of other women to fit the roles and ways of being that are considered acceptable and safe and that make everyone else comfortable.

Every once in a while, you see these social media threads that reverse gender roles, and it sounds so ridiculous that it's a great reminder that we're not nearly pissed enough about all this. A Twitter thread by A.R. Moxon (male) sums it up nicely by asking us to imagine that the patriarchy was actually a matriarchy and men were expected to accept what women have been accepting for generations.

> What if men needed a wife to own property for the next century or so.
>
> Or to open a bank account?
>
> And divorce is illegal.
>
> But no fear, 100 yrs or so after that there'll be a Constitutional Amendment declaring men are full people.
>
> It'll fail. But still—We've come a long way, baby!
>
> …What if we men knew there wouldn't be a male candidate for

presidency for 240 years, and even then he'd lose to the [female candidate], who'd been taped bragging about assaulting men during the campaign—but the media talked about what a scary time it was for women?[102]

Play this little game with any of the social gender norms and dynamics we've come to accept and in large part not even notice, and the ridiculousness is apparent. We simply wouldn't accept it. And no, I'm not suggesting we move to a matriarchal society that supplants men the way women have been supplanted for decades—that would just be perpetuating inequality and that's not the goal. Even picturing a matriarchy as the patriarchy but with women in charge is a patriarchal lens, and it's not what women want. So much of the world is built this way that it's almost impossible to imagine the world differently. But that is exactly what we need to do.

We need to imagine how the world could be different, better. Maya Angelou said, "When you know better, do better." We know better now, and it's time to do better.[103] We need to believe in our visions for that better world. To do that, we need to go inward and ask ourselves some big questions. We need to look inside, quiet all the noise and reconnect to our core. What kind of world do we want for ourselves and our collective children?

Humans, all of us, want meaningful lives. Many of us work really hard and are committed to our work, both inside and outside our

---

102   A.R. Moxon (@JuliusGoat), "What if men needed a wife to own property for the next century or so. Or to open a bank account? And divorce is illegal. But no fear, 100 yrs…" Twitter, April 23, 2019, 11:22 PM, https://twitter.com/JuliusGoat/status/1120890653754499072?s=20&t=GyCEKZCay-h_UDvmzjhGiA.

103   Maya Angelou (Verified) (@DrMayaAngelou), "'Do the best you can until you know better. Then when you know better, do better.' —#MayaAngelou," Twitter, August 12, 2018, https://twitter.com/drmayaangelou/status/1028663286512930817?lang=en.

homes. Sometimes the demands of work and the things we really care about are in conflict. I'd like a more meaningful life, more time with my loved ones, to contribute more to my community, but I'm so busy with work, and this dinner isn't going to make itself. What if we could take that very tenacity and follow-through that makes women so able to "do it all" and apply it instead to the things we really care about? What if we were as committed to the meaningful things in our lives as we are to our jobs and corporations and doing what's expected? That would be a life of purpose.

Let's break the word *purpose* down in a way that makes it easier to connect to.

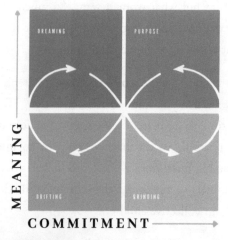

ADAPTED FROM: TAL BEN-SHAHAR, HARVARD

HOGIE2005, "COMMITMENT VERSUS MEANING," MY PURSUIT OF THOUGHT, 5 SEPT. 2019, ACCESSED JUNE 20, 2022, HTTPS:// PURSUITOFTHOUGHT.BLOG/2019/09/05/COMMITMENT-VERSUS-MEANING/.

This grid is an adaptation of Tal Ben Shar from Harvard (3)[104]

---

104   hogie2005, "Commitment versus Meaning," *My Pursuit of Thought*, 5 Sept. 2019, accessed June 20, 2022, https://pursuitofthought.blog/2019/09/05/commitment-versus-meaning/.

The purpose grid above changed my life. I always wanted to live a purposeful, meaningful life, but I'd only had glimpses of that at times when I had the freedom to follow my heart, which usually meant forgoing material rewards, doing volunteer work or outdoor leadership work, neither of which pays the bills. But then I'd rebound into needing to pay those bills and find myself in the grind, where I felt like I was doing what I needed to pay the bills but didn't feel particularly inspired or that what I was doing had meaning, to me or in the bigger picture. We all have times when we feel like we're in the grind, like we have the commitment to getting things done, without the meaning or inspiration.

Drifting times are when we just don't know what to do next, or even what is meaningful now. Maybe it's a time when what used to feel certain and meaningful no longer does. Drifting has a negative connotation in our production-driven world, but I've come to believe that in order to create the next thing, whatever it is, we need to spend some time not knowing exactly what it is or how to proceed. Uncomfortable, yes, but an important part of the creative process. If we jump right to the next thing without taking the time to drift in that creative void, we will often simply move to the next place of grind or recreate what is familiar and comfortable. Getting comfortable with not knowing, and trusting that it's a temporary state, gives us an opportunity to come to much more genuine and deep insights about what's next. Drifting is an important stage of the process.

And then there's dreaming. We often call people "dreamers" as a criticism in our society, as if dreaming is simply unproductive, unrealistic time-wasting. But dreaming is the place of invention and innovation. We can't get there by being productive or grinding all the time. We need to give ourselves time to dream. Dreams are the sparks that move us into purpose.

When I first saw this model, I admit I thought purpose was the goal, and I still do to a certain extent because I feel so good when I'm in that place. I absolutely want to live in that place of alignment where the work I commit to doing is meaningful and purposeful. But more and more I appreciate that the other places are important parts of the journey to get there. Being in the grind sucks, but it's a good motivator to look for meaning. We may not otherwise get ourselves in gear to do something different. Drifting doesn't produce anything, but if we can allow ourselves to not know, then the ideas and knowledge that do inevitably present themselves are authentic, rather than forced. And dreaming is where the beautiful, creative ideas come to us. Those can't be forced, and often they come to us when we are in a more resting mental state, when we're not trying so hard. We may not accomplish practical things in the dreaming phase, but when we do get into committed action with our dreams it can be magical. All four states are necessary and important stages on the road to purpose and meaning in our lives.

The reality is that conversations about purpose are inherently privileged because, if we're in survival mode, it's difficult to think about things like meaning and purpose, because meeting our basic needs and those of our families takes up so much of our bandwidth. That's why things like equal pay, paying traditionally feminized industries a living wage, fixing broken leadership pipelines, setting quotas for promotion of women, sharing the household labour, etc., are all so important, because if we can better meet our basic needs, then we can start dreaming bigger and have some energy left over to do something about it.

Where do we start to connect to the meaning we so desperately want to feel in our lives? Defining our values is a key piece of the puzzle. We often inherit values from our families and communities, and some of them fit and some may not. It can take some work to connect to the ones that really live in our hearts and minds. Our personal values point to what matters most to us. Many of us never articulate our values, but we feel it when they are trespassed. We feel an unease, a lack of alignment, a dissonance when we or someone around us acts in a way that is counter to our values. Our values are in us, whether we articulate them or not. Giving language to our values can be a powerful tool for understanding the world and making decisions. What would be different in your life if you filtered every important decision against your values and what matters most to you? Would you make different decisions? I know I do.

One of the exercises we do in all our women's leadership development programs is to articulate our core values. It's not complicated; you can do this yourself.

You simply find a list of values. I know Brené Brown includes an exercise like this in her book *Dare to Lead*,[105] and there's also a great values list available from the Center for Nonviolent Communication,[106] although that list uses the term *needs* instead of *values*. Think about that for a second. When we shift from calling these things values to calling them needs, human needs, their importance is even more highlighted. If we don't get these core needs met by living in alignment with our values, then we suffer, we know something is

---

105   Brené Brown, *Dare to Lead: Brave Work, Tough Conversations, Whole Hearts* (New York: Random House, 2018).

106   "Needs Inventory," The Center for Nonviolent Communication, accessed April 30, 2022, https://www.cnvc.org/training/resource/needs-inventory.

not right, even if we can't put our finger on what it is. The process of naming our core values, our core needs, is a way to create a compass in our lives that can guide us in all our decisions, big or small.

Below is the multi-stage process we work through in our programs for articulating values/needs:

1. Review the list of values and circle all the values that are important to you—don't worry about how many you have at this point.

2. Go through and cross off any that feel imposed or like "shoulds." Sometimes we carry values from our families or communities who expected us to live by certain values. Ask yourself if the values you have chosen are truly your own values or if they are values you've been told you should have.

3. Then highlight your top 10 list by choosing the 10 values that are most important to you.

4. Then prioritize further. If you could only have three to five, what are the most important ones? Prioritizing doesn't mean you don't care about the values that don't make your top three to five list. It just means some are more critical or important to you than others.

5. About combining: Sometimes, we have multiple words that mean essentially the same thing to us. Check in about which word is most resonant. In some cases, you may have one core value that is represented by two words (e.g., Meaning & Purpose).

6. For each value, assess how aligned you feel with that value

right now. You can use a scale of one to ten, one meaning you have no alignment to this value right now and ten meaning you are in full alignment. Are you living and leading according to this value? Are you making decisions in alignment with this value? How could you be more aligned?

Once you have your values and start reflecting on how aligned you are, keep your values somewhere you'll see them every day. Remind yourself every day that these are the things that matter to you, that this is how you want to live. And when it comes time to make a decision, check in. "Is this decision aligned with my values? In what ways? What would make it more aligned?" The reality for most of us is that not every decision we make feels 100% aligned with our values; there are still things in each of our lives that simply must be done, and we don't live in a place of absolute control and freedom to choose. But the question of what would make it more aligned is an important one. Most of us have more wiggle room on alignment then we believe we do. We may not be able to make decisions with complete freedom to align to our values, but we can get closer, each day, with each decision we make. And the very process of asking ourselves the question builds the habit of values alignment.

That's it. It's that simple, and yet it's a game-changer. One of the things that maintains the current system is our participation in it. In some cases, we don't even notice we're doing it because it's so common, so assumed, so invisible. Other times we accept the excuses of "this is just the way it is." Why? Why does it have to be that way? Who says it has to be so? The way the world is built is just something humans made up, and in the case of our modern world, it's something mostly men made up, for a time and circumstance we're no longer living in. So, we, as humans, can make up something different, something better, based on what we know now and based on what the world needs now.

It seems like a small thing to articulate and align with our values. But it's powerful, and it's grassroots. If every one of us stopped "playing the game" we don't really want to play, the world would change. If you're pissed off about Jeff Bezos and the billionaires getting richer every day while not paying their employees a living wage and not paying taxes, there is something we can each decide to do about that: don't buy from them anymore. Enough people do that, and the game changes. It's a quiet revolution that can happen when we simply choose values alignment in our own lives over the expectations of doing what we're "supposed" to do, or what everyone else is doing, or what we're told to do or be. When we stop going along to get along, we start asking different questions, and that leads us to take different actions.

Do we need more than a quiet revolution? Hell yes. The pace of change needs to be accelerated, and that will take activism on a larger scale, as well as people with the voice and platform and courage to advocate for systems change, policy change and culture change. But that doesn't discount the power of change and alignment in our own lives. That is the starting point and perhaps the biggest lever for change and more fulfillment in our own lives and the lives of our families and communities.

How you live matters. Your values and taking a stand for them matters. So many of us feel like all we do is work to make money, then spend that money on whatever, then go back to work again to make more, to spend it, and on and on. We wonder what life is all about. Is this it? Nope. It's not. It doesn't have to be. But if you choose more, if you choose meaning and purpose, then by that very choice you are swimming against the current, so expect resistance. Don't take resistance or pushback or people questioning you as an indicator that you've got it wrong; it's simply an indicator that you are disrupting, and disruption makes a lot of people uncomfortable, despite the rhetoric about how much we want it.

The biggest barrier to change is inaction, keeping things the same. As soon as you are different, as soon as you step out of line, the machine kicks in to push you back. It might be the people closest to you, the ones you thought would understand, who push back the hardest. And that's because unconsciously they know that getting out of line is dangerous. It's unpopular. And as humans, social animals, we know that being a dissenting voice, being unpopular, can threaten what is possibly our single greatest need: the need to belong. But somewhere along the line we traded true belonging for fitting in.

Brené Brown describes the difference between belonging and fitting in:

> The thing is that we are wired to be a part of something bigger than us so deeply, that sometimes we will take fitting as a substitute, but actually fitting in is the greatest barrier to belonging because fitting in says, "Be like them to be accepted." Belonging says, "This is who I am."[107]

So many of us have substituted fitting in for belonging because we fear that if we are our true selves, we'll be going against the grain and we won't belong. That's the thing that doesn't get talked about when

---

107   Brené Brown, *Atlas of the Heart: Mapping Meaningful Connection and the Language of Human Experience* (New York: Random House, 2021).

we talk about a life of values or purpose: the fact that it's disruptive and disruptors will always be pushed back into line, or pushed out altogether. Expect that, be ready for it, and don't take it personally. When others police you to conform, it is more about their fears than it is about you.

Your job is to cultivate the quiet places and the truly supportive people who will encourage you to follow your own heart, your own values, and your own path. I've never met someone who did that and regretted it.

At the Women's Leadership Intensive, we look at leadership as the desire to have a positive impact on your environment, and we see it as fundamentally an inside job. We start our leadership work on the inner circle of the diagram below, reflecting on our values, our life experiences, how we uniquely see the world and who we want to be as a leader. Only then do we work on the skill sets in the outer circle so that every leadership action we take is aligned. These explorations can be deep and sometimes surprising.

Take that inner journey and you'll start to feel a sense of purpose as you go about your daily life. In the day to day, I like to think about purpose as simply that place where what we have to offer—our unique strengths, perspectives and abilities—meets a need in the world, big or small. The need we are meeting could be just about the one person who is with us right now, or the one choice we are making to shop local, or the need we are meeting could be broader, a need for social change or justice. If we think about it that way, if purpose is just applying what we have to answer the call and meet the need we see, then we can find purpose all over the place, in actions big and small. We can find it in the most everyday things. Call

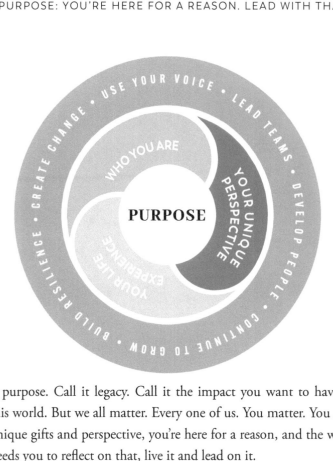

it purpose. Call it legacy. Call it the impact you want to have on this world. But we all matter. Every one of us. You matter. You have unique gifts and perspective, you're here for a reason, and the world needs you to reflect on that, live it and lead on it.

To do this requires us to question what we have been trained from childhood to do, which is conform and fit in and stay in line. We are taught to play and win at the game of status and achievement, of acquisition. The one with the most stuff wins. The world is not really set up for us to live our values and purpose, because the work of purpose is not about winning at that old game. The work of purpose is about playing a different game altogether, one where the playbook is not yet written, because we are writing it as we go.

PURPOSE

CHAPTER nine

Power: Time to change the game.

Feminism isn't about making women stronger. Women are already strong. It's about changing the way the world perceives that strength.

— G.D. ANDERSON[108]

We hear a lot about women's empowerment these days, there are tons of events and discussions about women's empowerment. But all that empowerment buzz has really started to bug me, and I've been trying to figure out why. Women's empowerment sounds good, and it's certainly something I'm in support of. So, why does it annoy me so much?

I think what it comes down to for me is that we're talking about empowerment but not backing it up with real action, like enforcing pay equity laws, demanding DEI transparency from corporations or fighting for legislation that provides and protects equality. How can we talk about women's empowerment while women's sovereignty over our own bodies and reproductive rights are under attack and anti-abortion laws are rearing their ugly heads again, not only in the U.S. but in other jurisdictions too? It feels performative and hollow, like a smoke screen. How can we have so many discussions about women's empowerment but still not have equitable sharing of actual power? It feels like bullshit.

Nobody cuts through bullshit with grace and intelligence like Nancy Wilson, founder and CEO of the Canadian Women's Chamber of Commerce (CanWCC). She and I talked about the word *empowerment* and why it's a problem:

> The word has always raised my hackles. And although a secondary definition has been added because of its ubiquitous usage, the original core definition of empowerment is "someone in power ceding or giving some portion of that power to someone not in power." And so really, when a corporation runs some women's empowerment group, the description of it is absolutely correct, but they shouldn't be patting themselves on the back. I mean, what they're doing is saying, "We hold all the power. You have very little or none. So, we're going to run this women's group. And in doing so, we will transfer some modicum of our power to you women." And that's absolutely what's happening. So, I mean, it is a correct description of what they're doing, but the way it's described is marketing. They're saying that this activity is actually increasing the power of women or solving some

kind of equity issue. Which it absolutely is not.

First of all, the premise is that it's a zero-sum game. Secondly, I don't consider human rights to be something that is ceded from one person to another. The system is set up a certain way and if the system gets modified, then we can all have power. It's not one person's cup fills up by emptying someone else's. So, the word empowerment, I do not like. And then it's just used across the board. It's like everything is women's empowerment, which means nothing is women's empowerment. Right?

And then once you get women's empowerment laid over self-help, which is really just laid over blaming the victim, I mean then really it's a perfect storm. It's exactly what the powers that be are hoping for because it's ultimately a distraction from systemic issues. And it focuses in a really negative way down to women, on what they are somehow lacking, and need to develop in order to be equal, to have the same opportunities. It's a vicious cycle.

And this distraction is used to prevent them from coming together as a community to actually hold people to account for those systemic issues. So, we are all distracted by working on ourselves, as opposed to coming together as a group saying, "Wait a second, how come this legislation is the way that it is?" Or, "How come we're not being paid the same amount in this company that's making so much money?" Instead, we're all working on our own career ladders individually.

What we need to do is look beyond the distraction of performative empowerment activities, and instead look at real power in our world. Whether we define power as political, military, economic, class, role, or position, I think the numbers clearly show that women do not have equal power in any of these systems because we do not have equal access, participation, opportunity or decision-making authority in any of them. If political power is about making decisions and setting the policies and laws that govern all citizens, then why should we not demand equal representation in choosing the rules we all follow? If economic power is about deciding how to allocate resources, including people, money and natural resources, should we not all participate in the decisions that affect us all? And if cultural power is about defining our reality, then why must some of us live in a reality that does not define nor fit us, one that we did not create or sign on for?

I will be happy to talk about empowerment when we start having real conversations about power, who has it, who doesn't and why.

Oxford University's Lexico defines empowerment as:

1. Authority or power given to someone to do something.

   "individuals are given empowerment to create their own dwellings"

2. The process of becoming stronger and more confident, especially in controlling one's life and claiming one's rights.

   "political steps for the empowerment of women"[109]

We are certainly making progress as women by both definitions. Yes, we have been "given" power to do things like own property, have financial resources of our own, vote, hold jobs, etc. Interesting

---

109   "Empowerment," Lexico, accessed April 30, 2022, https://www.lexico.com/en/definition/empowerment.

that the word "given" is part of the definition. Who gives power to whom? And why did they have it in the first place, while someone else did not? And yes, we are becoming stronger and more confident in controlling our lives and claiming our rights, decade by decade, generation by generation.

And yet. And yet, in and among that progress, we still live in a world where women primarily do not hold the positions of power or make the fundamental decisions that shape our organizations, communities and institutions. The conversation about what power is becomes the critical missing piece. We do have the capacity and ability to act and influence, and more of us are waking up to that and using our capacity and abilities. Though the original intent of feminism was to ensure basic human rights for women, the current wave of feminism is a social movement armed with broader social media tools and a focus on changing society for the better with equal opportunities and equity for both men and women, which does not exist right now.

You'll never hear me say that women aren't powerful. I've seen first-hand what women have created even in the absence of any position of power, in the absence of decision-making roles, in the absence of having an equal voice. It's astonishing what women accomplish every day, on every level, given our level of political, economic and culture-defining power and our ongoing exclusion from and under-representation in the traditional institutions of power. We have found ways to influence and work around all the gaps. Think about all the workarounds in your own life, all the ways you navigate the system to get your voice heard, to have your solution adopted, to have your reality acknowledged. To be seen. To stay safe.

We shouldn't have to go to extraordinary efforts to be safe or heard or seen or validated. We should have equal access to participate in the power structures and decision-making roles of our world. But the real game changer is in changing our very definitions of power. Gender balance and representation in politics or corporations is an important step, but we need to rethink our definition of winning and losing, and beyond that, our definition of the entire game itself. For women to enact the kind of change we're capable of, it's not about "winning at their game," it's really about changing the game altogether. Creating a new game that is better for more people, better for the environment, better for our children. Where there don't need to be winners and losers.

Let's talk about the ways we use power in our world today and how we define it. In her book *Cassandra Speaks: When Women Are the Storytellers, the Human Story Changes*, Elizabeth Lesser describes what she calls "old power" as the way we've historically perceived and used power.[110] And of course it's through a masculinized or patriarchal perspective. Old power includes the binary concept of strong and weak. In a strong versus weak mindset, the strong take the power, authority and decision-making, and the weak must accept it.

Old power is competitive. The idea of competition is an interesting one. I see it as an overdone value. Some competition can be motivating for many of us. It may draw us forward out of our comfort zones or be just plain fun at times. I'm not saying human beings don't have a drive to win sometimes—we do. And I'm good with that. But when we make everything a competition, it creates a binary environment where only some people can be "winners" while

---

110   Elizabeth Lesser, *Cassandra Speaks: When Women Are Storytellers, The Human Story Changes* (New York: Harper Wave, 2020).

others are "losers." It also doesn't acknowledge the absolute inequity in the playing field. Any playing field, every playing field. Winners aren't necessarily winners because they are somehow better or more qualified or work harder than losers. Many winners are simply better resourced. We see that in sports, in business and in politics.

Yes, it's theoretically possible that any Canadian child can make it to the NHL if they are talented enough. But that doesn't take into account the time required to practice, the money required to play on teams and compete for positions, the transportation to practices and games, the family support, the access. Oh, and the fact that the NHL is only for boys, and mostly white boys at that. There are professional women's hockey leagues, but on at least one of the sites I explored, they were clear that the players didn't actually get a salary, just a share of the prize if they won. So yeah, that sounds like a career decision most of us wouldn't be able to make. I'm not sure my landlord would be good with an arrangement where I only paid the rent when my team won a game.

This plays out in business and other positions of leadership and power as well. The outcry is strong when we try to implement things like quotas or affirmative action policies. People cry that we should simply hire the best person for the job, the one most qualified. What does that mean? The one with the most education? Not everyone has equal access to that. The one with the most experience? We also don't have equal access to that. The one who has done these kinds of jobs before? Well, that simply repeats the pattern of having the same demographic of leaders we've had before. Great for them. Not so great for the rest of us. Jamile Cruz, founder of I&D 101, says it well:

In diversity, equity and inclusion work, we talk about establishing targets or quotas. People will need to get comfortable with affirmative action concepts. Certain formats of "affirmative action" were always present, but they were used towards white men and sometimes white women.

When you switch to say affirmative action towards under-represented groups, that's when executives get uncomfortable, because you're asking them to share the power. On that front, I feel a bit more optimistic because if we do push towards the 30%, once we get there, in a group of 10, then we're three, we're no longer the only one. There is power in numbers.

Then we're going to stop with the "She is the first Black woman to have this position" and move on to, "Look, Jamile is here and brought Belinda and Laura to be part of this group." Then we can look at the changes that have happened since they've joined the organization. If the culture is open and inclusive, and people get the opportunity to actively participate and contribute towards business goals, we will see the positive impacts of a diverse team.

Canadian Prime Minister Justin Trudeau created a gender-balanced cabinet upon being elected for the first time in 2015. When asked why he did it, his response was simply, "Because it's 2015."[111] Right? Anyway, there was an uproar. Were those women qualified? Did they only get the job because they were women? The irony was incredible. Men's over-representation had never been questioned this way. If we in fact believe that we've been operating in a meritocracy, then does

---

111 "Trudeau's 'Because it's 2015' Retort Draws International Attention," *The Globe and Mail*, November 5, 2015, https://www.theglobeandmail.com/news/politics/trudeaus-because-its-2015-retort-draws-international-cheers/article27119856/.

that mean people actually believe that (white) men are truly better at pretty much everything? How else could we explain their over-representation in every leadership category?

Back to the idea of competition. If competition is our way to approach everything, it's a big problem. It's like having a cooking competition where only one competitor gets pots, or food. The resource gap makes a huge difference in any competition. And one of the most important resource gaps is time. When I work with women leaders, they are often on the brink of exhaustion. They are busy all the time. They go from work to home to caring to work to more work to raising kids to making dinner. The idea that they could compete for leadership positions, run for office, create, write a book, become the next thought leader is not impossible—women have always found ways to do all of those things. But it is harder because all of that requires time, along with other resources. Time to think, to create, to build. Writing a book is a great example. To write a book, you need time to focus and think and actually write—never mind the money to publish. Many writing courses recommend that you lock yourself in a room for hours or days at a time so you can focus and write. How many women do you know who can do that? Most women would laugh outright at the idea.

Are there more male "thought leaders" than women? Probably, because they have more resources, and more time. The question is, who cooked their dinners and raised their kids and bought a birthday card for Aunt Martha while they wrote the book and built the empire? I once had a participant in our online women's leadership course refer to her husband's business success and say, "I've always said that the reason he was able to be so successful is because he had an amazing executive assistant." How many women have an amazing executive assistant? Imagine what we'd all accomplish if we did!

Shonda Rhimes, African American producer, author, screenwriter and creator of the TV show *Grey's Anatomy*, sums it up well:

> I'm not fully present at work. I don't think anybody who has kids is fully present at work…The idea of pretending that we have no other life is some sort of fantasy out of the 1950s, where the little lady stayed at home…I don't have a little lady at home. So if I am excelling at one thing, something else is falling off. And that is completely OK.[112]

Most women simply don't have the luxury of single-minded focus.

Another quality of old power is over-valuing individualism. It's another myth, the myth of the "self-made man." I'm not saying there aren't self-made people out there, I'm not saying you didn't work hard to get to where you got, but I am saying it's rarely a solo effort. People with more support get further in the world. That's not rocket science.

I used to work in outdoor education and did my fair share of rock climbing, kayaking and adventuring of all kinds. To this day, being in the wilderness is what I love to do. In my twenties, I was making more of a career of it, so by default I hung out with a lot of dudes—mountain climbers, extreme kayakers, etc. Some of them went on to be the high-priced keynote speakers who come into your corporate meeting to convince you that climbing a mountain is just like turning a big profit next year or creating a successful company. Here's the thought that kept dogging me the whole time I was working in

---

112   Judy Berman, "Shonda Rhimes Already Knows What You're Going to Watch Next," *Time*, January 10, 2022, https://time.com/6132884/shonda-rhimes-profile/.

that space. Not how heroic the whole thing was. Not wishing I could be like them. Nope. How individualistic and *selfish* it was. That's what I kept seeing and hearing. Just plain old simple selfishness. Did they climb the mountain to advance humankind (like their keynotes would have you believe)? It didn't seem so from my vantage point. They did it because they wanted to and they could. Did the billionaire playboys of 2021 go into space to further science and save the planet (like they would have you believe)? I don't think so. They did it because they wanted to, and they had the resources to. There are lots of ways to further science that use a lot fewer individual resources and have way more positive impact. They did it because they wanted to. Individualism. Selfishness. Period. And that's what an overfocus on individualism does. It builds a society where what an individual wants and can get, based on their individual resources, is the pursuit. In many cases, that gross over-consumption and selfishness is revered and even held up as something to aspire to. We've framed it as a desirable lifestyle.

That's a pitiful use of resources in a world where we have more than enough for everyone, but we haven't done a good job of sharing. Remember, as Vicky Saunders, founder of SheEO, says, "The scarcity thing is really bad, right? There's enough for everyone. It just isn't well distributed."

Elizabeth Lesser's book *Cassandra Speaks* also discusses how those old power values that have gotten us into so much trouble need to be balanced out with new power values, and I couldn't agree more. She talks about partnerships and collaboration, the valuing of relationships, empathy and communication, the sharing of encouragement, listening and inclusion. I don't know about you, but that sounds way more like the world I want to live in. Just saying it gives me a sense of relief and breathing room. I have to believe there is more to being human than the idea that the person with the most stuff wins.[113]

The game of status and achievement as a way to "win" at life has become a driving force. Acquisition keeps us busy enough to ignore our inner voices, values and calls from the world. This pursuit of status and achievement has been so compelling and so damaging, on a personal and global level. I'm not suggesting a world without achievement, without using your talents to excel. Not at all. I think that's brilliant and joyful. But when we chase achievement and status to the detriment of values, or purpose, or doing the work of being a global citizen, it becomes a problem. We find ourselves with systems like the ones we have today, where capitalism is king, where "the market" drives decisions about things like the cost of housing, even to the detriment of so many who can no longer afford a place to live. We say, "It's too bad, it's just the way the market works." Meanwhile, humans created the market economy system, and some humans can create something different, better.

Maybe you've tried to step away from the capitalistic model that drives so many of us to work and spend our way through life, being too busy or too tired to pay attention to much else. Maybe you've asked yourself some of the deeper questions, like, "What really matters to me?", "What do I value?" or "What kind of world do I want to leave for the children?" Maybe you've started the process of reflecting on the world around you and asking the why questions. *Why is the world set up this way?* Maybe you've even asked the deepest questions of all: "What am I here to do?" "What contributions can I make?" "How can I use what I have to do good?" Those are import-

---

113   Elizabeth Lesser, *Cassandra Speaks*.

ant questions, necessary questions. And once we start asking them, just working or spending money doesn't fill the holes anymore, and we can't pretend it does. If we ask those questions and then do nothing with them, we just go through the motions of life on autopilot, wondering what it's all for.

Asking ourselves those hard questions is the place in time where we shift from external power—the trappings of the external world, status, achievement, material possessions—and into a place of internal power—humanity, meaning, purpose, wisdom. Janet Hagberg writes about this shift in her book, *Real Power: The Stages of Personal Power in Organizations*. She talks about when we make the shift away from external power by status and achievement into the inner world of reflection, purpose and wisdom. When we make this shift, we often hit what she calls "the wall." The wall is made up of both internal and external resistance. The inner resistance often comes in the form of self-doubt: *Who am I to take this path less travelled? What if people don't understand me or like me or approve of me? What if I'm wrong?* The external resistance comes as pushback. When you rock the boat, someone will try to set it straight again.[114]

Brené Brown calls putting yourself out there "entering the arena."[115] When you want to create something, when you put yourself out there, she says the only certainty is that you'll get your ass kicked. You can't stick your neck out and not become a target for someone, and not be plagued by your own self-doubts at times.

The other thing Dr. Brown says, and she jokes that it's set her free

114   Janet Hagberg, *Real Power: Stages of Personal Power in Organizations* (Illinois: Waveland Press, Inc., 2003).
115   Brené Brown, *Daring Greatly.*

and made her quite dangerous, is that if you are not also in the arena, creating, trying to build something, and also getting your ass kicked, she's not interested in your feedback.[116] That is a critical thing to hold on to. Yes, you will get pushback, but you get to decide how and if you take that feedback in and take it on. That has been huge for me. It's allowed me to simply disengage from abusive conversations, or no longer have conversations with people who are trying to convince me that equality is actually bad for women, or bad for the world. Yes, that still happens. I'm more conscious these days of who is also in the arena, exploring new territory and also getting their asses kicked, because inherently new territory means we don't always get it right.

I do get to choose where I put my energy and who I surround myself with, but this doesn't mean I only hang out with people who agree with me. That's a whole other danger zone. But I can have boundaries. If respectful exchange is not happening, I don't have to stay. If someone doesn't recognize me as equal, I don't have to stay. If someone gaslights me or actively discourages my perception of the world, I don't have to stay.

The two things that I recommend to anyone who is questioning whether the way we define power or success in our society is working for you is one, go hang out with other people who are also questioning. It's way easier if we do it together. More fun too. We need community to explore new ideas together and organize thoughts and actions. And two, get clear on your boundaries, understanding where your line is, where you too can say, "I'm not interested in your feedback."

---

116   Ibid.

CHAPTER ten

Presence: Sometimes you need to fight to be heard.

I raise up my voice—not so that I can shout, but so that those without a voice can be heard.... We cannot all succeed when half of us are held back.

— MALALA YOUSAFZAI[117]

You better not compromise yourself. It's all you've got.

— JANIS JOPLIN[118]

---

117   "Malala Yousafzai: 16th Birthday Speech at the United Nations," Malala Fund, July 12, 2013, https://malala.org/newsroom/malala-un-speech.

118   Derek Norcross, "The Little Girl Can Sing," *The Orlando Sentinel,* April 6, 1969, https://orlandosentinel.newspapers.com/image/224193186/?terms=%22the%20little%20girl%20can%20sing%22&match=1.

Throughout this book, we've talked through so many examples of how women's voices are not only not heard, but actively discouraged. I see this happen in multiple ways. Some of the discouragement comes from within, the internalized gender expectations that we not rock the boat, that we serve others, that we "be nice." Some of it comes from others shutting us down. I don't know one woman who can't think of an example or tell a story of having been shut down by someone.

How many times has someone said something you disagree with or something that felt like an aggression or micro-aggression—a sexist comment, a racist comment—and you railed against it internally but said nothing in that moment? Then later, you thought of all the things you could have, should have said. Don't be too hard on yourself. There are good reasons why we do this, safety being first and foremost. Women have become experts at adapting to keep ourselves and others safe. A simple example is how many adaptations and mitigations women make to simply walk down the street at night: phone on, headphones out, panic button on the car keys ready, mindful of what we're wearing and who's around us, and on and on. Keeping quiet is one way we protect our physical safety, and certainly, we have many examples of how women are physically threatened with sexual violence, domestic violence and political assaults on our bodies and sovereignty, such as the abortion bans springing up in the U.S. In other cases, the threat is that of social exclusion, a threat to our need to belong, or a threat of verbal, mental or emotional abuse, gaslighting, being ridiculed, or being called names reserved exclusively for the purpose of shutting up and dismissing women, from the more subtle "emotional"—meant to indicate our ideas have no merit—to more overt terms like "bitch." We have a collective history and individual lifetimes of conditioning that teach us to monitor and mitigate for threats and that being quiet and compliant is one way to keep safe.

In some cases, to stay safe or to make our way, we've learned to actually side with our aggressors or oppressors. Women can become complicit in our own oppression by becoming agents of the patriarchal system to be on the side of power and thus secure our positions in those power systems. We feel this as the deepest betrayal from one another. And the saddest part is that it doesn't work because even if we play the boys' game and uphold the system, we still aren't truly included there, not as ourselves, only inasmuch as we play along. It's an illusion. And the cost is high, both personally and to other women.

When we do find and use our voices, we may have the confusing experience of being actively not heard, such as the example I shared about answering a question about the weather on that Outward Bound course and having both the male participant and my male co-instructor behave as if I hadn't spoken at all. We all have examples, some subtle, some not.

That was the day I knew I was done with co-instructing with men. I don't paint all men with that brush, and I had some truly wonderful experiences co-leading trips with men, but that experience was common enough that it was an easy choice for me to make. I just didn't want to deal with that dynamic anymore. I wanted to co-lead trips with women. And when I did, it was so freeing to not have that gender binary dynamic playing out in the background all the time. We could just be who we were.

The term "mansplaining" describes experiences like this, where men explain things that women already know and have already said, where a woman speaks but is ignored and then a male colleague says the exact same thing and gets heard. Sometimes it feels like we're not even there. It's a disturbing experience.

And then there are the systemic barriers to women's voices, like the fact that there are often no women in the room when decisions get made; it's hard to have input when you're not there. When there are women present, we are more likely to be the "only" or the minority. There's been some great research on what it's like to be an only. The only woman. The only racialized person. The only person with a disability. The only LGBTQIA2S+ person. Bottom line, it's really hard work. You represent a perspective and lived experience that is different from that of the dominant group, and it can be really hard to communicate that. Even if you're a brilliant communicator, and you have to be if you're an only, your voice may not be recognized, your voice may not be heard. Often, the dominant group doesn't actually want to hear what you have to say because it disrupts the dominant perspective, and disruption and change are, at best, hard work.

Jamile Cruz, founder and CEO of I&D 101, shares a story of how persistent this problem is and how one only does not solve the problem nor change the system for everyone else:

> I was with a friend in Rio, we met when we were 14 going to school to get our first technical degree and then we went to different engineering schools, but we both studied electrical engineering. She's Black. Everybody always asks us if we're sisters. She married a Black man who first studied engineering then medicine. He works as a doctor today. They have two kids.
>
> When the search for schools for their kids started, I was visiting, and we had a conversation about the availability of schools with

Black representation… in the student group and in the faculty and administration. With the financial access they currently have, the search focus was for the best education, just like our parents did. If we asked our parents: "What was the thought process when you put us in private school? Were you searching for representation? Was that even in your head or were you just searching for the best school?" All our parents would answer the same thing. They were searching for the best school.

They knew we would face some bullying and issues because essentially the three of us and our siblings were the only ones or one of the few Black kids at our schools. We have "managed" the situation because we needed to get the best education. And you can see the results of us getting through it and building the lives we have today – a good education is a critical factor. The social mobility we have was provided by our parents pushing hard and getting us into those schools.

But the thing is, my friends are essentially in 2022 going through the same experiences as our parents. On the search for the best school now they're faced with, "Wow, our kids are also going to be the only Black kids." When they chose a school, they had a conversation with the directors. They went to visit and the only Black people that they saw during their visit were working in the kitchen. Did my friends have other choices if they wanted to access the best education? They didn't. So, they ended up in this school, their kids will go through the same experience that we did. So, when you think about this cycle, we're 40 years later, what has changed?

As an only, you may be considered a "diversity hire." Boards and executive teams now facing criticism for their lack of diversity are feeling the pressure to proactively seek out diverse members. Depending on which cluster of companies you looked at, women in 2021 represented about 23% of board members and 18.2% of executives.[119] Another way to look at that 18.2% is it's about 1.69 women executives per organization,[120] which means a lot of onlys! When you're a member of the dominant group, you get to represent your own point of view and experience, but when you're an only, you are expected to represent your entire group. Only woman in the room—what do women want? Only Black person in the room—speak on behalf of all Black people. When you're in the majority group, you can stick to your personal perspectives and opinion, and that is enough. Your credibility isn't questioned or scrutinized. Nobody asks if you're qualified, or if you only got the job because you're a diversity hire. You don't come in having to prove yourself; your credibility is assumed. The difference in the demands and requirements for those in non-dominant groups just to participate cannot be overstated. It's way more work just to show up.

Things get better when you're not the only one or one of the very few. The demands persist, but now you may have others who validate your experience or share the burden. U.S. sociologist and Harvard Business School Professor Rosabeth Moss Kanter hypothesized back in 1977 that when an organizational minority assumes a presence of one-third or more of a group, it can influence or "tilt" the culture

---

119   Andrew MacDougall et al. "Report: 2021 Diversity Disclosure Practices—Diversity and Leadership at Canadian Public Companies," Osler, October 13, 2021, https://www.osler.com/en/resources/governance/2021/report-2021-diversity-disclosure-practices-diversity-and-leadership-at-canadian-public-companies.
120   Ibid.

of the overall group.[121] Working with this theory, we would need to have 30% of any nondominant group in order for them to tilt the culture or enact real change and have their voices truly heard. When we have less than 30%, the risk is that we get assimilated; there are simply not enough of us to create culture or systems change. The energy required to resist assimilation is immense. It often requires us to be driven by a strong personal mission to be that dissenting voice, and to do that over and over again.

Even in the face of all of this, the reality is that the world needs to hear from women. In fact, I'm not sure we'll manage if we don't. It's time for change, systemic, even revolutionary change, and times like that are never easy.

Sometimes we underestimate or underutilize the voice or resources we do have. We put our heads down and work hard. It took a long time for me to say to myself, *Okay, you're okay. You have a roof over your head, and you know who you are. If you're not going to speak up now, then when? What are you waiting for? How much do you need to have done before you can claim a space to say what you think? And who are you waiting for? Who do you think is going to get this done? Are you waiting for someone exceptional, someone so much smarter, more articulate, more resourced, braver?* And that's when the mantra came to me: If not you, then who? If not now, then when?

It feels safe to stay quiet, but we come to regret it at some point. When you look back on your life, do you want to say that you shut up and did what they told you? Fuck that. Standing up and out is

---

121 Rosabeth Moss Kanter, "Some Effects of Proportions on Group Life: Skewed Sex Ratios and Responses to Token Women," *American Journal of Sociology* 82, no. 5 (1977): 965–990, https://www.jstor.org/stable/2777808.

not easy, but at a certain point, the opposite isn't either—it too has a cost. At least in stepping up to your true voice and leading as *you*, you don't have to compromise yourself. Finding the courage to show up is hard. The risk is real, and we feel alone. So, what does it take to find your voice and show up as *you*? The trick is not to do it alone.

Each one of us does need to find, validate and approve of our own voice, but it's way easier to do that when we're surrounded by people who also encourage and validate our points of view instead of discouraging and invalidating them. That voice inside us needs nurturing to grow stronger and overcome a lifetime and a history of being told to keep small.

There's a lot to be said for women's networks, but I think we need to go beyond networking to build community.

> Specifically, a network is a set of relationships that links individuals such as friends, acquaintances, and coworkers to each other. Networks are open chains of connections characterized by the fact that when networks intersect, they become one larger network. Networks are expansive and open without having a concept of membership, little expectation of mutually supportive interaction beyond the first or second connection. Networks establish loose or weak bonds between people.

> Sometimes, companies or organizations use the term network or include the word in a group name because networking – helping people who might be mutually helpful meet – is the purpose. Often, such a defined entity is really a community, such as a corporate Women's Networking Group.

> Remember that a community is a mutually supportive, self-per-

petuating group with purpose and structure. If you are looking for belongingness and close bonds, you want to find a group (or groups) where you have a shared purpose with the other participants and a structure that facilitates connection.[122]

Both create connections, but community is where we do the work. Nancy Wilson, founder and CEO of CanWCC, works hard to create community:

> Community is a tricky one and I'm definitely still learning about how to build a community and engage people. And I think that the whole idea of bringing together a group online and building a community has become super transactional because of how social media works these days. So, we all know that and expect that we should be able to join communities for free. And most people I think understand that it's not really free, we're paying for it with our data, and our thoughts, and our consumer behavior, and all of that.
>
> So, the first stumbling block is, how do you cover the cost of a private community, if that's what people need and want? People need money in order to operate private communities where that data is actually not monetized. And so with CanWCC, although we started very early on with a Facebook group, I did not want our community to be on Facebook because I wanted people to really feel like they had a safe space to talk about what was happening, and what I did know is that there was no way for us to control what Facebook took from its own

---

122 Kathy Edersheim, "Community or Network: What's the Difference?" *Impactrics*, July 7 2021, accessed June 20, 2022, https://impactrics.com/community-or-network-whats-the-difference/.

platform, and there was no way for us to fight that. That's one side of things.

The other side is, in order to get people to really engage, I think that you need to, as a community member both in these Zoom meetings, at events and stuff, but certainly also in the posts online if you're doing it that way, you have to be willing to be really vulnerable yourself, and role model what you want the community to look like. And I'm okay with doing that. I also know that my experience, my life, my background, my skin color, I have got a lot of privilege going on. So, I want to position my stories in the right context, making sure that I understand and I'm sharing these stories knowing that there's a lot of privilege behind these stories. I'm not saying, "This is the worst that's going on out there." I know that I've enjoyed a lot of privilege.

We create community as a place to share perspectives, share vulnerability, build trust, engage in real dialogue, show up, listen and include. But there are also some practical actions we take in community to support one another and serve the common mission. Organizing, advocacy and activism are perhaps most important and more possible when we work in community. And there are other actions we each can take as well. The three we talk about most in our women's leadership programs are coaching, mentoring and sponsoring.

Coaching

Coaching at its core is using questions to help someone design a solution that is aligned to meaningful change. Let's break that down. We use questions in coaching because coaching assumes that the person we're talking with is creative and resourceful, and if given an opportunity to reflect is more than capable of tapping into their inner knowing and intelligence to determine their own best path forward. We need this deeply in the world. There are so many forces out there telling us who we need to be, what we need to do, creating scarcity and fear, and driving us to just keep performing without really considering what it all means, what it costs and if it's actually what we want. Coaching is a core leadership skill in a world where people want to do more than what they're told, in a world where people want to be thoughtful, values aligned, collaborative and creative. Coaching supports the achievement of our personal and professional goals and growth. We need coaching, but it alone is not enough. We also need mentorship and sponsorship.

Mentoring

Mentoring is when a person with particular experience provides you with guidance and advice. We are starting to see more women's mentorship programs popping up in organizations, and they can be game-changers. The real benefit of being mentored is that you get to learn from someone else's path, strategies, mistakes and lessons learned. This saves us an immense amount of personal trial and error and can keep us from falling into pitfalls that are known to someone else but may not be known to us. The other thing that can be game-changing about having a mentor is the notion that someone believes in and supports *you*. There is a person in your corner, and that can make all the difference.

Sponsoring

Sponsoring means someone advocates for your success, promotes you directly and uses influence, power and networks to connect you

with assignments, roles and access. This is possibly the most important piece for women. Men have been doing this for one another
forever. It's been the "old boys' club," where men sponsored one another to get jobs, meet the "right" people, have access to the places
where decisions get made, and basically open all manner of doors
for one another and create opportunities. I'm not advocating that
we take that model and create "the old girls' club" and exclude a
bunch of other people. Absolutely not. Let's not repeat the mistakes
of the past. What I'm saying is that we should proactively sponsor
those who do not have sponsors, who have been excluded from access and opportunity, and support them with whatever resources we
have. Women have been getting more coaching, although a lot of it
is geared toward coaching women on how to fit in and make it in the
man's world, and that needs to change. Now there's more mentoring
of women too. But this sponsorship piece makes the difference at a
very real level. It can get you the job, the client, the opportunity, the
access. And without that, we'll continue to struggle for the resources
we need to reach our potential, let alone the resources we need to
lead change.

The most important thing I want you to walk away with here is this:
no matter where you are, really no matter where, there is someone
looking at you and wondering how you got there, wishing they knew
what you know or could be where you are. We often don't think of
ourselves as leaders, coaches, mentors or sponsors, and we really need
to start. I cannot encourage you enough to do two things:

One, seek out a coach, a mentor, and a sponsor for yourself. This
may be one person, or several. If you want your path to wherever
you're going to be easier—and trust me, you do—get some actual,
practical support behind you. It can be hard to ask for these things,

but it's time to believe that you are worthy and make the ask. Be choosey. Make sure your coach, mentor and/or sponsor is actually working with and for you. Just like the word "leader," these other roles can be in name only. Be selective. Choose someone with whom you belong.

Second, offer coaching, mentoring and sponsorship to someone else. Learn how to do these things, build the skills, spend as much time learning these core leadership skills as you might have spent learning your functional capabilities. Once you are in a leadership role, regardless of title, if you want to lead, then whatever functional or technical capabilities you have are half your job. The other half is the skillset and capabilities of leadership, and those skills take just as much effort to master. As you're learning and mastering (don't wait to be perfect!), make it part of your personal leadership mission to proactively support other women coming up, particularly those who don't look like you, particularly those who haven't been given this support. Don't wait until you "arrive" to help others move forward. Someone once referred to it as "send the elevator back down" to pick up more women, from wherever you sit. As Audre Lorde, who dedicated both her life and her creative talent to confronting and addressing injustices of racism, sexism, classism, and homophobia, says, "I am not free while any woman is unfree, even when her shackles are very different from my own."[123] Let's recognize and share the resources and access we have, big or small, and proactively support one another to get where we each want to be. As Rupi Kaur says, "when one rises, we all rise."[124]

---

123   "(1981) Audre Lorde, 'The Uses of Anger: Women Responding to Racism.'"
124   Rupi Kaur (@rupikaur_), "When one rises we all rise. when someone wins…" Instagram, October 17, 2019, accessed June 20, 2022, https://www.instagram.com/p/B3VhHIbh1nY/?hl=en.

CHAPTER *eleven*

If not you, then who?
If not now, then when?

To all the little girls who are watching this, never doubt that you are valuable and powerful and deserving of every chance and opportunity in the world to pursue and achieve your own dreams.

— HILLARY CLINTON[125]

As the impact of the COVID-19 pandemic continues to be felt, closing the global gender gap has increased by a generation from 99.5 years to 135.6 years.

— WORLD ECONOMIC FORUM[126]

125 Katie Reilly, "Read Hillary Clinton's Concession Speech for the 2016 Presidential Election," *Time*, November 9, 2016, https://time.com/4564480/read-hillary-clintons-concession-speech-full-transcript/.

126 "Global Gender Gap Report 2021," World Economic Forum, March 30, 2021, https://www.weforum.org/reports/global-gender-gap-report-2021/digest.

Let's go back to my simple definition of leadership: having a positive impact on your environment and the people around you. By this definition, you are a leader. I believe that. And it's become my mission to help you believe it too. Because when you believe it you start taking actions that align with that belief, and that, my friend, will change the world.

Here's what writing this book has taught me. Actually, when I think about it, my whole life has taught me this: I'm not special. I am not a genius. I'm actually pretty average in pretty much every way. So that's a relief. Because knowing that makes me realize that anything that gets done in the world probably gets done by other kind of un-special, average people like me, and that gives me so much hope. We don't need to be exceptionally gifted or talented to do something. We just need to get about the business of doing whatever it is we think matters. The paradox is that, although we are all just human, each of us is unique, and the contributions we can each make are also unique. Every single one of us matters. For real.

IT'S NOT ABOUT BEING SPECIAL.

Years ago, when we ran Paddle to a Cure and we raised almost $1 million for breast cancer research and education by taking survivors and supporters into the wilderness on sea kayaking expeditions, I met so many people who told me about their similar ideas. They too wanted to raise money for causes close to their hearts, or they had wanted to do big expeditions or follow dreams. And it made me realize that my idea wasn't particularly special. Lots of people were thinking about it. The difference was just in the doing. Of course, that takes resources, support, skill in whatever area you're creating in, but it also takes sweat, time and commitment. It takes putting one foot in front of the other when you're not exactly sure what you're doing each day. And it takes putting yourself out there for something, not knowing how or if it will work.

I'm not saying that's easy or even simple. We don't all have time. We don't all have the resources, skill sets or confidence in our areas of interest or passion. To this day, the number one thing so many women who come to the Women's Leadership Intensive programs want to gain is confidence. That's still a huge piece of the puzzle. And we all have our reasons why we don't put ourselves out there, and those reasons are real and valid. And yet we all need to do what we can with what we have.

USE WHAT YOU HAVE.

The truth is that I got really lucky. First, I was born in a country with really solid access to education—thank you, Canada and all countries who value and provide high-quality public education. And I was able to function well in the education system. I could figure out what they wanted and deliver. My parents supported me and believed that I could and should be as educated as I wanted to be, and they had the will and ability to sacrifice in order to save money to help support that education.

Later, I stumbled into a job and place that I loved and where I could explore who I really was: outdoor leadership. In many ways, I should never have gotten that job. I was unqualified and inexperienced; someone recognized something in me, enough to offer me an opportunity and help me get there (sponsorship). And somewhere in me, I heard a call to try this scary new thing, and I was willing to put myself in a situation where I had to learn absolutely everything. I took the risk and then buckled down to learn and build my competence.

As I mentioned earlier, the more my feminist perspective took root, the less likely I thought it would be that I would find a male partner who would treat me as equal, fully respect my humanity, and, frankly, not hold me back or hold me down. It didn't seem possible. Then I met Shane. It was not love at first sight; it was curiosity, friendship, doubt and a bunch of other messiness. But eventually, his humanity and his vulnerability to be himself made space for me to trust him. It has not been idyllic or perfect—it's been up and down like every other relationship—but I can count on him to be fully human and to give me the space to be the same. He supports me and trusts me to make my own decisions about my life, my work, my views on the world, because we are partners, we are side by side as equal humans.

FOCUS ON WHAT MATTERS.

The next lucky thing was the creation of Paddle to a Cure: Journeys of Hope. Could we do expeditions (something I loved) but in a way that contributed, that was accessible and inclusive? A way that was not about rugged individualism, but about community? Connecting that work to the breast cancer movement made perfect sense to me, as I had a personal connection through my own mom. I knew the women I wanted to work with, but I wasn't sure they'd want to do it. Maybe they'd think it was crazy or just not possible. So many unknowns, all the volunteer hours and unpaid work. But every single one of those women said yes. Sarah said yes, even with two young daughters at home; Ally and Annie said yes, even though none of us was really in a financial position to do unpaid work for months at a time. This taught me the unbelievable power of saying "yes" even when you don't know how something is going to go, or how to make it happen, saying "yes" to the whisper inside ourselves and to the brave and bold ideas of the people around us.

SAY YES.

The gifts to me from Paddle to a Cure were many. Five summers spent sea kayaking with amazing women and some truly wonderful men. Making a contribution to a cause that matters to me personally and to so many others. Making some of the best friends of my life. But I also learned some really important truths, one of which was that great ideas are not the thing that makes shit happen in the world. That idea that started Paddle to a Cure was a spark, 1% of what made it actually happen. The other 99% was doing the work, and doing it as a community. Showing up, trying stuff, getting it right, getting it wrong, and, in our case, doing all of that together, as a community of volunteers, a community of women.

The second big learning that propels me forward to this day, 20+ years later, was how a community of women could organize using feminist principles to create a very successful, purpose- and values-driven organization that can balance many priorities at once. It was my first experience with what might be called a 360-degree or multi-stakeholder organization. We had many stakeholders and many priorities. We had the goal to raise money for breast cancer research and education, but we also had the equally important goal of creating safe, brave, accessible, inclusive sea kayaking experiences for everyone, from a person who had never paddled before to someone who was an expert. We had sponsors, partners, local communities we travelled through, the wilderness environment, volunteers, past participants, families and so many more stakeholders that we considered, and we worked hard to create win-wins around the whole circle. It was complicated but rewarding.

We balanced process with outcomes. Our community planning meetings throughout the year were epic events in organizing. Hours around our living room, potlucks to beat the band, babies, debates, discussions, ideas and agency. Each person's voice had space, and we experienced the complexities and rewards of shared decision-making. It was not easy, but it was rich and life-affirming and in the end got us to better decisions. It was magic.

EMBRACE THE COMPLEXITY.

All that and more set me up for where I am now. It gave me the confidence and support to change course when I was almost 50 and doing just fine. I had a thriving leadership development and coaching practice, some lovely partners and great clients. I was making a fine living and working on projects I mostly enjoyed with people I mostly enjoyed and had a pretty good lifestyle. I could have ridden that train to retirement. But the world just wasn't sitting right with me, nor was my place in it. Was this really what I was meant to do with my one beautiful life? Was I okay with just keeping on? I knew in my heart I was not. There's this quote from Elastigirl in the movie *The Incredibles* where she says, "Girls, come on! Leave the saving of the world to the men? I don't think so. I don't think so."[127] I knew that the world needed women, and with my background in leadership development, I could support women to lead as themselves, and in that way make a contribution.

I took some time, years, to go from knowing something needed to

---

127   *The Incredibles,* directed by Brad Bird (2004: United States: Walt Disney Pictures and Pixar Animation Studios).

change to figuring out what was next. I continued my work and, after every project, I reflected and realized, nope, that's not the thing for me. It's fine, but fine is not what I'm looking for. I kept working because I had bills to pay. I kept reflecting, I just paid attention. I knew I wanted to do something that mattered more, but I didn't know what.

It was actually a male friend, Tim Arnold, who looked me in the eye and reminded me that my sweet spot was women's leadership; that had become apparent in the Paddle to a Cure years. I had been avoiding it, to be honest, hoping to just tweak what I had been doing rather than completely reinvent myself. And I knew that stepping out into the world of gender equity would be to step onto the battle-field in ways that scared me because I'd seen how hard that could be and the kind of backlash that could come. But when Tim said that to me, I knew he was right.

I went back to my feminist roots and did the work of scanning the data. Where were women now? What progress had been made? What was still to do? When I realized the numbers for women weren't get-ting better at a significant rate, and our children were going to have to fight the same bloody battles I had as a young woman, that's when I got into action. Most notably, hearing about girls and young wom-en facing the same comments, discrimination and sexual harassment I had faced decades ago made it impossible to turn away. I would be damned if I didn't at least try to leave this place better than I found it.

ASK YOURSELF THE HARD QUESTIONS.

I fully believe young people should be leading *right now*, not when they get to be middle-aged and just like all the other leaders that went before them. No. We should be inviting them to lead now, while their perspectives are *different* from the norm, because that's what will shake things up—and things definitely need shaking. Right now, things are tough for young people. They don't have money, they have student debt, they are expected to get in line in their early careers, pay their dues, do what they're told and emulate the people in front of them instead of being themselves. Young men don't have healthy role models for masculinity. Toxic masculinity is everywhere in our culture. Watch a movie and ask yourself who we expect men to be. Watch TV. Do you see good role models for men?

Girls and young women still face discrimination, sexism and misogyny at every turn. They still don't see themselves represented in leadership. Young women in particular, are still taught by media that their core value is to be pretty and sexually available. Young women can't walk down the street or into a meeting without being objectified, sexualized or expected to perform feminized tasks like taking notes and organizing social events. This even applies to executives. I can't tell you how many executive teams I work with where the few women on the team are still the ones doing the housekeeping tasks, minute-taking, and social organizing work of the team. And now that many organizations are waking up to the demand for diversity, equity and inclusion strategies and action plans, it is mostly women who are doing this DEI work, often on the sides of their desks, as their companies tell them it is so important but then fail to pay them for the extra work.

I see my role now as coaching, mentoring, sponsoring, and clearing an easier path for those who are coming next. No, I do not want another generation of women to have to fight for abortion rights. No, I don't want to leave universal day care for subsequent generations to figure out. Let's get this done now. I'm tired of waiting. This is the work for all of us. Maybe you feel like you didn't contribute to or benefit from the unequal systems and institutions of our world right now. Even if that's true, it's on us all to roll up our sleeves and make as much progress as we can, to make it easier for people to lead in new and better ways, because the world needs it. Badly.

BRING OTHERS WITH YOU.

The truth is, it is up to you and me. It always has been. It has to be you who takes your place in creating the world you want for yourself and your children. It won't be easy, but it will be fulfilling. It will be a life worth living and a story worth telling. And if we do it together, then the road will be way less lonely.

> *Our strategy should be not only to confront empire, but to lay siege to it. To deprive it of oxygen. To shame it. To mock it. With our art, our music, our literature, our stubbornness, our joy, our brilliance, our sheer relentlessness—and our ability to tell our own stories. Stories that are different from the ones we're being brainwashed to believe.*
>
> *The corporate revolution will collapse if we refuse to buy what they are selling—their ideas, their version of history, their wars, their weapons, their notion of inevitability.*
>
> *Remember this: We be many and they be few. They need us more than we need them.*
>
> *Another world is not only possible, she is on her way. On a quiet day, I can hear her breathing.*
>
> — ARUNDHATI ROY[128]

---

128   Arundhati Roy, "Confronting Empire," *The Nation*, February 20, 2003, https://www.thenation.com/article/archive/confronting-empire/.

Acknowledgements

As we all do, I stand on the shoulders of giants. My own thinking and writing has been greatly informed and influenced by so many researchers, writers, speakers and thinkers, and that continues to this day. I keep learning more and changing my views. The more we learn, the more our thinking and behaviours evolve; thank goodness. These are just a few of the amazing, courageous women who I hold in such high regard. They speak the truth and even today we know how risky that can be. Thank you to Sarah Kaplan, Elizabeth Lesser, Nancy Wilson, Glennon Doyle, Caroline Criado-Perez, Katrine Marçal, Vicky Saunders, Malala Yousafzai, Brené Brown, Gloria Steinem, Kimberlé Crenshaw, and so many more. Thank you for your leadership.

Personally, I need to thank my family. My partner Shane Doyle is a true feminist and ally. We work through this shit on a daily basis.

Thanks for always being willing to have that conversation. And even more so, thanks for all the laughs along the way. My son, my heart, Gabe Doyle, is the next generation and everything I care about and work for in this world is my attempt to make it better for him and his peers, of all genders. Thank you to Louise Walker who has been with me through thick and thin. Like, really thin, sometimes. I am thankful to walk this lifetime alongside you.

My parents, Bruce and Loralie Clemmensen, gave me the gift of education and independence. I hope I have honoured both. Thank you. I love you.

Our team at WLI is a privilege to work with every single day. I feel lucky to hang out with you all. Claudia Valle, you make everything we do better. Brianne Ligori, your coaching has been invaluable. Caitlin Cooke, your creativity amazes me. Jamile Cruz, you have taught me so much. Ellen Duffield thank you for your research and for believing that my work and WLI matters deeply. Cheryl Sutherland, Karen Malone, Lisa Deguire, Linda Walker, Lindsay Johnson, Wendy Brookhouse, thank you for sharing your considerable expertise with our community each year.

To all the women who have participated in our WLI courses over the years, thank you. Thank you for trusting us with your development and your friendship. I cannot express how much I believe in each one of you. You are the leaders of today and the future and that gives me so much hope.

A few people have been instrumental in getting this book done. Allison Fallon of Find Your Voice, taking your excellent course got me a book outline without which I could never have gotten anywhere on this project. You are a good human and I'm grateful to have met you. Julie Broad and Elissa Graeser at Booklaunchers held my hand through editing, layout and all the other things I didn't know I didn't know about writing and publishing a book. You are damn good at what you do. Alyssa Burkus, Tim Arnold, and Shikha Gandhi thank you for the test reader feedback and all your support as I went through this new journey of writing. Your guidance and positive support have been invaluable.

Writing a book is a privilege and one I don't take lightly. I know I'm lucky and I am thankful every day.

Made in United States
Troutdale, OR
11/15/2024

24875409R00116